Code with Confidence

-Python for Beginners

A Step-by-Step Guide to Ease into Programming and Boost Your Analytical and Creative Thinking.

By Albert Rutherford

www.albertrutherford.com

Copyright © 2023 by Albert Rutherford. All rights reserved.

No part of this publication may be reproduced, stored in a retrieval system, or transmitted in any form or by any means, electronic, mechanical, photocopying, recording, scanning or otherwise, except as permitted under Section 107 or 108 of the 1976 United States Copyright Act, without the prior written permission of the author.

Limit of Liability/ Disclaimer of Warranty: The author makes no representations or warranties regarding the accuracy or completeness of the contents of this work and specifically disclaims all warranties, including without limitation warranties of fitness for a particular purpose. No warranty may be created or extended by sales or promotional materials. The advice and recipes contained herein may not be suitable for everyone. This work is sold with the understanding that the author is not engaged in rendering medical, legal or other professional advice or services. If professional assistance is required, the services of a competent professional person should be sought. The author shall not be liable for damages arising herefrom. The fact that an individual, organization of website is referred to in this work as a citation and/or potential source of further information does not mean that the author endorses the information the individual, organization to the website may provide or recommendations they/it may make. Further, readers should be aware that Internet websites listed in this work might have changed or disappeared between when this work was written and when it is read.

For general information on the products and services or to obtain technical support, please contact the author.

I have a gift for you…

Thank you for choosing my book, Statistics for the Rest of Us! I would like to show my appreciation for the trust you gave me by giving The Art of Asking Powerful Questions – in the World of Systems to you!

In this booklet you will learn:

-what bounded rationality is,

-how to distinguish event- and behavior-level analysis,

-how to find optimal leverage points,

-and how to ask powerful questions using a systems thinking perspective.

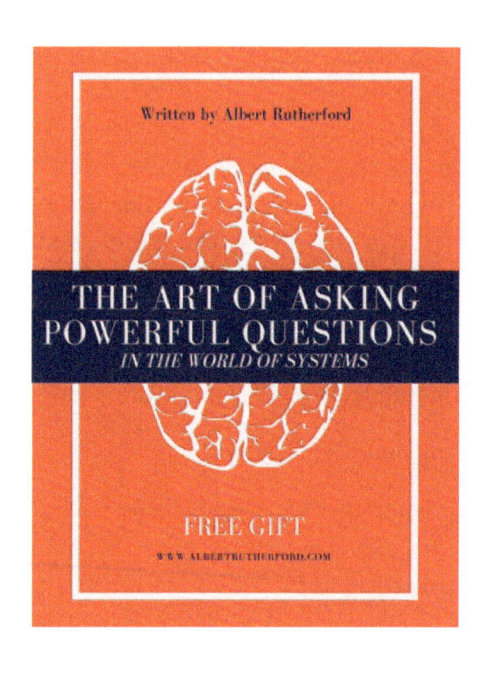

Visit www.albertrutherford.com to download The Art of Asking Powerful Questions in the World of Systems

Table of Contents

Introduction	11
1. Setting Up Your Computer	15
2. Understanding Python Syntax	21
3. What Are Variables?	43
4. Control Flow And Conditionals	57
5. Python Data Structure	77
6. Python Functions	95
7. Input And Output Operations	107
8. Modular Programming	117
9. Small Python Projects	125

Final Words	141
Before You Go…	143
About The Author	145
Reference List	147
Endnotes	159

Introduction

Whatever your reason for deciding to go with Python, it is a splendid choice. Among various programming languages, Python stands out as simple and beginner-friendly.

But the question is, why would you choose Python and not something else? Since you've invested in Python, you probably already know the answer. But here are a couple of data points that will affirm you are on the right path.

As per a 2018 survey of young professionals, 48 percent of them preferred Python, with the R being the second option at 38 percent[i]. In addition, as per IEEE Spectrum's top programming languages of 2022, Python is the number one choice![ii]

If I ask you, what is an industry that is experiencing rapid growth and excitement, expected to have a profound impact on our future? You will likely say it is Artificial Intelligence (AI) or Machine Learning (ML). And you won't be wrong. Experts in coding conclude that Python is better suited for both AI and ML.

People use Python everywhere, from web development to data analysis and visualization to automation and scripting to cybersecurity and the Internet of Things. How does Python impact you daily? It powers many things you use on the world wide web. Every time you browse on the internet, check your Instagram feed, shop online, stream videos, or access online banking, Python is the likely backstage master.

Programmers love Python because of its simplicity, compatibility, strong community support, and intuitive design. It is cost-effective and seamlessly integrates, making it popular.

As a beginner in computer language, the user would want the coding process to be easy, simplified, readable, and flexible, with easy applications. Python holds all these qualities; its simplicity and readability contribute to reduced program maintenance costs. One can simply write a Python code as plain text and execute it. The execution of codes is much faster than the other programming languages available.

This language has become increasingly popular among users and programmers in recent years. Its ranking among the top computer languages globally is clear. One of the major reasons for this demand is its easy accessibility on online platforms. The Python interpreter and extensive standard library are freely available for major platforms. It supports modules and packages, promoting code reuse and modularity. Don't worry about these terms. We will cover everything in the upcoming chapters.

It would amaze you to see the online community that exists to provide support and guidance to learners of Python. The developer community has a lot of information about Python in articles, tutorials, and blogs. When any product or commodity has support from big corporates, these products grow faster. The buyers and users all build trust because of its association with reliable and established moguls in the market. For example, Oracle sponsors Java, Microsoft supports Visual Basic and C#. Amazon web services, Google, and Facebook are the biggest supporters of Python. Google has a major role in boosting Python in computer programming, having used it for many of its applications and on multiple platforms. Google Cloud has a platform specifically for Python applications, offering options like serverless, VMs, Kubernetes, and custom hardware.[iii]

Python is popular because it is inclusive, free, and constantly improving. I'll go as far as saying what it doesn't have is yet to be established.

And we have Python's original creator, Guido van Rossum, to thank for this. In 1991, Guido van Rossum, while working at CWI, published the source code of Python's interpreter as open-source on alt.sources, a Usenet group. This move was significant at the time, as the business models for language development were still uncertain. Open-sourcing Python played a crucial role in its success. In 1994, version 1.0 was released, and they created a dedicated Usenet group. During this time, other dynamically typed and interpreted languages emerged, but Guido's invitation to the National Institute of Standards and Technology (NIST) allowed him to promote Python and attract key contributors, shaping the language's future.[iv]

What's the most interesting thing of all? Python was a hobby project for Guido. A hobby that has changed the world.

1. Setting Up Your Computer

Before we get started, there is the minor matter of making sure Python operates on your computer. Fortunately, it's a straightforward process.

Python, a versatile programming language, supports multiple platforms, including Linux, Mac, and Windows. While it comes pre-installed on macOS and most Linux distributions, it is advisable to download and install the latest version to stay up to date.

This chapter shall outline the process of how to set up Python and understand the process behind it. The following instructions will help you start your coding journey in no time:

Python on Windows

- Open the Microsoft store, either on your computer or through the browser.
- Search for Python from the search option on the website.
- Select the Python version you want to choose (it is recommended to choose the

latest version, i.e., Python3) and then select Get.
- Once Python has finished downloading and the installation process is completed, open Windows PowerShell.
- Once the PowerShell is open, the user can confirm the installation of Python3 by entering *Python – version* or simply writing Python and pressing enter.

Your Python is in good shape and is ready to run codes when you see the >>> display on your window.[v]

Python on Linux:

- The requirement to install Python on Linux:
    - Your computer should run on Debian or Fedora OS with a minimum of 2GB RAM (4GB preferable) and 5GB of disk space.
    - You also need to have access to sudo (Sudo User DO) on the system you want to install your Python on Linux (the sudo command lets the users temporarily elevate existing user accounts to have root advantages).
- To check the Python version on Linux:

- Since Python comes pre-installed on most of the Linux distributions, you can check the Python version by running *python – V* or *python – version* command on your function window/terminal/console.
- If there is no Python installed on your computer, the terminal will reflect Command "python" not found, but can be installed with:
  sudo apt install python3
  sudo apt install python
  sudo apt install python-minimal
- When you already have Python installed on your system, the output will say
  Python x.y.z version.
- First, you can install Python from the Package Manager.
  - Syntax: sudo apt-get install python3.
  - Respond by typing Y and pressing enter to continue.
  - The package manager will automatically get Python installed within your system.
- Second, build from the Source Code.

- - Pre-requisites—git, gcc, and make installed on your system.
  - To get the source code, you can clone the latest Python source code from the repository GitHub, the official website of Python.
- Once the latest Python version is downloaded, the user has to extract the tar file to install Python.
- Configuration of the script should be executed.
- Understand and follow the steps to install Python on Linux and finish the installation.
- Undertake verification of the installation.

Regardless of the operating system (OS), you can obtain the appropriate version of Python by visiting the official Python website and downloading the suitable 32-bit or 64-bit version for your OS and processor. This is typically a recommended option, but there are also alternative methods for specific operating systems.[vi]

Python on macOS

People who own Macs should feel happy, as Python is already installed on their computers. It is still recommended to upgrade to the new version of Python regularly.

- To check the current version of Python:
    - Open terminal from utilities.
    - Type *python – version*.
    - Press return.
- Download Python for Mac:
    - Open the website python.org/downloads.
    - Opt for downloading Python.
    - Double-click the package file.
    - Proceed through the installation.
    - Option to download.
- It is recommended to not delete the older Python version from your Mac. Since Mac utilities are made to use the older version, deleting it could cause errors.
- The few best options for Python editor on Mac are:
    - IDLE (integrated development and learning environment) comes along with the downloaded Python file.
    - Although it is good enough for beginners, there are better options available online, like CodeRunner,

PyCharm, Sublime Text, Whisk, Dropzone, etc.[vii]

Another option is to use the Anaconda distribution, which provides Python, along with a wide range of pre-installed packages and libraries. Alternatively, if you prefer a more minimal installation, you can use Miniconda, which allows you to install only the required packages.

Now that we have installed Python and understand the value it holds in the field of computer language, we will get into learning the language that powers the virtual life around us.

We will start slow by learning about Python syntax and gradually move toward more complex topics.

2. Understanding Python Syntax

You want to code in Python. The very first step is writing a line of code. However, you must follow certain rules so that the Python interpreter knows exactly what you are trying to convey. Not following the rules would most likely result in bugs. And, of course, you don't want that to happen.

For example, in the English language, "Let's eat Grandma" and "Let's eat, Grandma" have completely different meanings (thank God for that!). How you structure a line and use the right syntax in Python are also extremely important.

That being said, unlike other languages, Python was designed to be very readable. In some ways, it mimics natural language.

Without getting too far ahead of ourselves, look at the following lines of code. You might broadly understand what the code is supposed to do. Even if you don't, no worries. That's what we will learn.

Number_1 = 10
Number_2 = 15

Number_3 = Number_1 + Number_2
print("Sum of", Number_1, "and", + Number_2, "=", Number_3)

As you might have guessed, the output for these lines of code will be: *Sum of 10 and 15 = 25.*

Essentially, the first and second lines assign a variable a value, in this case, an integer. The third line is another variable, which is adding the first two variables by using the "+" operator. The Print function gives the final output mentioned above. We will cover variables, operators, etc. in greater detail as we go along.

While the codes do get complex, with a little bit of practice and the tips and tricks we will cover, you will be writing such codes (and hopefully more complex ones) in your sleep.

1. Python Line Structure

Let's start with understanding how a line of code or a statement works.

Python line structure includes both physical and logical lines. A physical line is essentially each line of code. A logical line, however, is what the Python interpreter reads as a line of code. The following code is considered to have one physical line and one logical line.

number_list = [1,2,3,4,5,6]

It can also be written in the following manner, and in this case, it has five physical lines but only one logical line.

number_list = [1,
2,
3,
4,
5,6]

As a best practice to make the code more readable, it is recommended to write a single logical line on each physical line. In other words, one physical line should cover the complete logical line. In our example, the first way of writing is better than the second.

It is also interesting to note that in Python, the end of a statement is simply the end of the line without the need to add something like a semicolon (;), unlike other programming languages, such as C or C++. As you can see in the statements above, once we have written the desired code, we simply move to the next line.[viii]

2. Python Multiline Statements

While we can wish life was simple and a single line of code could suffice, a single statement never really changed the world. There are programs that you probably use every day that run into millions and billions of lines of code. Professionals estimate the Microsoft Windows operating system to have around fifty million lines of code. If that's not enough, they estimate Google to have two billion lines of code that drive its search engine, maps, Gmail, YouTube, etc.[ix]

More lines of code do not always mean a complex program, although a complex program can almost always be expected to have a lot of lines. Don't believe me? During the writing of this book, yours truly came across a code with 1022 characters to add two numbers. A long code, but not a complex one.

A new line of code in Python means a new statement. However, there may be cases where you have long lines of code and you want to break it to make it easier to read, so using the backslash character (\) can be useful. So, we can write the above line as:

number_list = 1,
2,3,4,5,6

Another way of doing this is to continue expressions onto the next line within parentheses. Generally, this is the preferred way to go about it, making the expression:

number_list = (1,
2,3,4,5,6)

Both these ways give the same result: *(1, 2, 3, 4, 5, 6)*

Sometimes you may want to combine two statements into one physical line, so adding a semicolon (;) between the two statements does the trick. So, the following is also another way of writing the statement instead of having them in separate lines.

Number_1 = 10; Number_2 = 15

Using a semicolon to put multiple statements on a single line, however, is generally discouraged for the sake of readability.[x]

3. Python Comments

Recall our example of a billion lines of code in the previous section. How would anyone navigate or understand the code if someone is looking at it for the first time, or the coder is revisiting the code after a long time?

Guido van Rossum, the creator of the Python programming language, once said, "Code is more often read than written." Therefore, the code needs to be understood by people other than the developer.

There is a best practice that is used by all programmers to ensure the code remains easy to navigate and understand. One can annotate computer programs by adding human-readable descriptions that explain what the code is doing and why it is doing something.

What this means is adding comments within the code to make it easier to understand, explaining any assumptions you might have made, or even highlighting why you structured the code in a certain way. Comments help with code maintenance, bug discovery, and code understanding.

There is a neat way to add comments in Python. A comment begins with a hash or a pound character (#). All characters after # till the end of the physical line are part of the comment, and the

Python interpreter ignores them. You can see how it is used below.

> *# The two lines below assign a value to variables Number_1 and Number_2*
> *Number_1 = 10*
> *Number_2 = 15*
>
> *# The following line assigns the sum of the two variables in a third variable*
> *Number_3 = Number_1 + Number_2*
>
> *print("Sum of", Number_1, "and", + Number_2, "=", Number_3) # The print function displays the output*

As you can see, anything added after the # character is not considered by the Python interpreter, irrespective of whether it is inline or in a different line altogether.

Also, style guides for Python code recommend comments to be a maximum of seventy-two characters. In case you exceed this limit, using multiple lines for your comments is the way to go.[xi]

4. Python Docstrings

Don't you hate it when the instructions that come with your latest purchase are not clear and seem to be written for someone pursuing their PhD in rocket science? Well, that's the purpose comments solve. They are meant for developers to understand the code and are generally written informally with no strict format. By developers, we mean folks who design, write, test, or maintain the code and can include programmers, engineers, and software architects who work on different aspects of the code.

While the comments make sense to them and help them understand the code, if you are an end user of the code who wasn't involved in its development, comments alone aren't going to help, which is where Python docstrings, or documentation strings, come into the picture.

Python docstrings are intended for users of the code and follow a structured format. Docstrings generally follow a format of describing the purpose, arguments, and return values of a code. Written in triple quotes (''' or """) immediately below the definition of a function, they are also used to create formal documentation.

Sticking to our example of adding two numbers, the following shows the difference between how docstrings and comments would normally be written.

Docstrings	Comments

def add_numbers(x, y):
"""
  Add two numbers.
 	
  Arguments:
    x (int): The first number.
    y (int): The second number.
 	
  Returns:
    int: The sum of x and y.
"""
  result = x + y
  return result
 	
# Using the function with numbers 	
Number_1 = 10
Number_2 = 15
sum_result = add_numbers(Number_1, Number_2)
	def add_numbers(x,y):
	  # Add two numbers
	  result = x + y
	  return result
	
	# Using the function with numbers
	Number_1 = 10
	Number_2 = 15
	sum_result = add_numbers(Number_1, Number_2)
	print(f"Sum of {Number_1} and {Number_2}:

print(f"Sum of {Number_1 } and {Number_2}: {sum_result}")	*{sum_result}")*
Output: *Sum of 10 and 15 is 25*	

Another important difference between docstrings and comments is that docstrings are retained at runtime. This is helpful if you are going through a large code with thousands of lines and you come across a function (in the table above we defined the function *add_numbers*) but don't know what it does. You can access this docstring during runtime using Python's built-in help() function. So, if you type help(*add_numbers*), the docstring will show in the output without you having to search for it like looking for a needle in a haystack.

If you have a question about what the "f" you see in *print(f"Sum of {Number_1} and {Number_2}: {sum_result}")* means, well, you have a keen eye. We will be covering f-string in the coming chapters, but good work noticing it.[xii]

5. Python Indentation

Giving space in real life is very important. Now, you want your space and I want mine, but guess what, Python wants its space too. In other words, Python loves indentation. The word indentation refers to the space provided at the beginning of the line to denote a block of code.

A block of code is a collection of lines of code written in the same indent and executed line by line. Essentially, they are a group of statements that are logically grouped and executed as a unit. Here is an example.

```
x = 10
y = 20

if x>y:
    print("x is greater than y")     # This is a block of code
print("y is greater than x")

z = x + y
print("z")
```

In the above example, the "if" statement by itself has no meaning unless there is something that happens as a result of the "if" statement, like the "print" statements below it. If you want the "print" statements to be a result of the "if" statement, they will need to be indented.

The way to read this block of code is if x>y, then print "x is greater than y," else print "y is greater than x."

You may have also noticed the use of a colon (:) in the example above. A colon holds a lot of importance in Python and is a crucial part of the Python syntax. It is used to indicate the beginning of a code block and is used for conditional statements (if, elif, else), loops (for, while), and defining functions and classes, among other things.[xiii]

Just as you never forget your morning tea or coffee, don't forget to add a colon when starting a block of code.

Other programming languages like C and C++ use brackets to define a block of code, while Python uses indentation. Python automatically provides indentation when you go to the next line of the block code. Ignoring indentation has dire consequences. Well, not dire, but you get the gist. So, ignore indentation at your peril.

Now let us look at an example explaining indentation:

Code with indentation:	Code without indentation:

if 5>4:
    print("Five is greater than four")
Output: *Five is greater than four*
 	
Comment:
print(Five is greater than four) is in the intended block
	if 5>4:
	print("Five is greater than four")
	
	Output:
	File "demo_indentation_test.py", line 2
	    print("Five is greater than four!")
	    ^
	IndentationError: expected an indented block
	
	Comment:
	Error occurred because we skipped the indentation

6. Python Multiple Statements in One Line

Multiple statements in one line can be used using semi-colons. In Python, one can simply write multiple lines of code and run the complete code using a semi-colon (;). Unlike other programming languages, a semi-colon in Python is used to denote the separation of statements rather than the termination of a statement.

Let us look at the example where we are executing three different statements of code in a single line using a semi-colon.

Code:

 # Three statements separated by a semi-colon

print('Hi'); print("Bye"); print('''Welcome''')

Output:

Hi

Bye

Welcome

Although multiple statements in a line are possible, however, it is not encouraged to use them. Multiple statements in one line lowers readability and breaks uniformity. Therefore, we should only use the multiple statements if it enhances readability.

7. Python Quotations

In Python, users can use single quotes('), double quotes("), or triple quotes(''') to denote string literals. Before I get into this further, let's see what I mean by strings.

While these strings are a little different from the ones big businesses might pull to get things done, if you learn Python, you won't need to pull any to get your next exciting opportunity.

On a serious note, strings are created in Python by writing a text or a group of characters quoted in single, double, or triple quotes. Using the same example as above:

print('Hi'); print("Bye"); print('''Welcome''')

The text 'Hi', "Bye", and '''Welcome''' all represent strings since they are in quotes. As you can see, any sequence of characters that is put inside single, double, or triple quotes is called strings. Here is another example –

First_name = "Ben"
Last_name = '''Franklin'''

Full_name = First_name + " " + Last_name

print(Full_name)

This will give the following output:

Ben Franklin

Furthermore, the following example will help illustrate how Python treats things with and without quotes differently.

print("two") # This is fine since this is in quotes

The output for this will be two.

However, the following will give an error saying *NameError: name 'two' is not defined*.

print(two)

In summary, Python can read and understand strings with one ('), two("), or three (''') sets of quotes. An important thing to remember is to be consistent with your quotes. Whichever quotes you have used at the beginning of the string, you must end with the same quotes too.[xiv]

8. Python Blank Lines

Blank lines in the code are primarily there to improve code readability. To illustrate this, we use an example we used earlier, but with and without blank lines.

With blank lines	Without blank lines

def add_numbers(x, y):
  result = x + y
  return result
 	
Number_1 = 10
Number_2 = 15
 	
sum_result = add_numbers(Number_1, Number_2)
print(f"Sum of {Number_1} and {Number_2}: {sum_result}")
	def add_numbers(x,y):
	  result = x + y
	  return result
	Number_1 = 10
	Number_2 = 15
	sum_result = add_numbers(Number_1, Number_2)
	print(f"Sum of {Number_1} and {Number_2}: {sum_result}")

While this is a simple example of a few lines of code, the blank lines marginally enhance its readability. Imagine a code with hundreds or thousands of lines, however—blank lines would surely enhance the readability significantly.[xv]

9. Python Identifiers

You seem like someone who would have close friends. Now, imagine they didn't have any names. How would you save their phone numbers, look them up on your favorite social media platforms, or call them out in a crowd?

You can do all this easily only because they have names, right? That's exactly what identifiers are. Identifiers are nothing but the name given to the entities in the Python program.

Identifiers are user-defined. This means that you can give them the name of your liking, unlike the names of your friends or cousins or maybe even yours. This helps to differentiate one entity from another.

The way we have names for people, animals, plants, etc., we similarly have identifiers for different variables, functions, classes, or modules within Python programming.

These terms may seem fancy and technical, but you'll realize they aren't once we cover them in the subsequent chapters. And once you get a hang of these, revisit this section to see how much you've learned and grown.[xvi]

Coming back to the topic at hand, let's start with a simple example:

_a = 2

A = "two"

for_example = 3

example1_2 = 4

print(_a, A, for_example, example1_2)

Here '_a', 'A', for_example, and example1_2 are identifiers.

While this seems easy, certain rules need to be followed when it comes to naming conventions for identifiers.

a. An identifier may only begin using alphabets (A-Z, a-z) or an underscore (_). An identifier can also contain numbers provided they are after a letter or an underscore (_).
b. An identifier may be multiple words, but they need to be connected by an underscore (_).

This is also called the snake case convention. It involves writing words in lowercase and separating them with underscores.

c. Python is case-sensitive, so test, Test, and tEST will be considered three different identifiers.

d. We will also need to be mindful of a few keywords that are reserved words in Python and can't be used as identifiers. They are used to define syntax and perform operations.[xvii]

Therefore, not everything can be made an identifier. I am sure you would not have a friend whose name is "orange" because of obvious reasons. Similarly, in Python, a few words are reserved and cannot be used as identifiers. While we will cover these in greater detail later, they are listed here for future reference.

False	*None*	*True*	*break*	*and*	*as*	*class*	*def*
assert	*else*	*elif*	*del*	*finally*	*in*	*or*	*pass*
raise	*nonlocal*	*try*	*while*	*with*	*return*	*yield*	*not*
from	*global*	*if*	*import*	*lambda*	*except*	*is*	*for*
continue							

Except for True, False, and None, all of the keywords are in lowercase and must be written that way. These are not valid variable names, function names, or other identifiers.

If any of the keywords is used as a variable, the error message will be displayed. *SyntaxError: invalid syntax.*

This chapter has a lot of information, but it is a good starting point as we go deeper into the world of Python programming. It is important to also practice what you learned to make sure you retain everything. Starting with this approach will prepare you well for the upcoming chapters.

As Aristotle, the Greek philosopher, said, "Well begun is half done."

3. What Are Variables?

One of the major utilities of any programming language is that it can process data. And to process data, variables are essential. They can store data for processing and can also work with the results of the data processing. Before we get into variables, let me take you down your childhood memory lane.

Remember how your mother used to ask you to bring something from the kitchen, and they would know the exact location of the specific item stored within a specific container kept on a specific shelf? It needs a lot of practice and a good memory to remember such precise information. I don't know about you, but I still don't know where I keep the charger of the laptop I am working on, which is about to die any second.

Oh wait, I just remembered! I can continue.

One can imagine variables as containers on the kitchen shelves with labels on them. These labels represent the variables' names. The content of the container is the value the variable holds.

Fortunately, Python has a much better memory than I do, and it has variables that play a key role in storing and referencing information. Variables are like containers that can store data values.

Python is a dynamic language, and it simplifies the process of storing information irrespective of the nature of information assigned to the variable. Variables are easy to create and get created as soon as we assign a value to them. Let's start with an example.

x = 4
country = "Japan"

Here, we have created two variables: country and x. We assigned the string value "Japan" to the country variable and integer value 4 to the x variable.

If we have assigned the value of "x" as four, we have declared the value of "x." Now, wherever the "x" variable is used, we will get the assigned value 4 automatically. Similarly, across the code, "country" will mean "Japan" unless it is changed. That's right. Variables can be re-declared even after they have been declared once.

Variables can be declared with any name, including alphabets such as "a," "aa," or "abc."

 # Declare a variable and initialize it

```
x = 4
country = "Japan"
print(x)

# Redeclare the variable

x = "four"
print(x)
```

The output for this will be the following:

```
4
Four
```

The value "Four" for "x" will remain until the variable is declared again with a different value. In other words, Python considers the latest declaration. This process is also called variable reassignment. Generally, it is not recommended, as it can lead to confusion and make the code harder to understand and maintain. Therefore, choosing meaningful variable names and using separate variables for different purposes is recommended, something we will cover in the next section.

Naming of Variables

Continuing with our trip down to the childhood kitchen, it is important to ensure that any content is stored in an appropriate container. Some items have to be stored in airtight containers, while liquids have to be stored in bottles to prevent leakages. Choosing the right container is critical to preserve whatever we try to store.

Similarly, there are certain sets of rules to be followed while naming Python variables.

- "A variable should start with a letter or an underscore character.
- "Variable names should only contain letters, numbers, and underscores.
- "Variable names cannot have spaces or special characters.
- "Usage of descriptive names is suggested (neither too short nor too long).
- "Use of lowercase letters and underscores to separate different words is recommended."[xviii]

Differences between Identifiers and Variables

You might be wondering about the difference between an identifier and a variable. These are related but slightly different concepts. It can get a little confusing, but read on to understand these better.

Identifiers, as the name suggests, helps identify a user-defined item, which can include variables, functions, classes, or modules. Identifiers follow the rules mentioned above.

Variables, on the other hand, are a type of identifier, but they are used to store data. Variables will hold data like numbers, strings, lists, etc.[xix]

You would be right in saying that all variables can be identifiers but not all identifiers are variables. Let's take a look at a few examples to understand this better. In the following example,

def calculator(length, breadth): # Calculator is an identifier (function identifier to be precise, but let's not worry about that right now)

   *area = length * breadth*
   return area

 # Area is a variable that is storing the result of a calculation

length = 10
breadth = 20
 # Length and breadth are variables that store numeric values

print(calculator(length, breadth))

Hopefully, the example helps clear up things.

Types of Data

Let's talk about the different types of data. Your kitchen has different containers for various types of ingredients, such as dry, liquid, solid or semi-solid food items, etc. Similarly, in Python, every value stored in a variable has a data type.

Data types represent the categories of multiple data, which are segregated to avoid confusion and help understand the purpose of each data type. Different variables can be represented by multiple data types, like integers, lists, numbers, strings, dictionaries, tuples, floats, etc.

I will briefly introduce you to the different data types in this section.

Few examples of the data types:

1. String (str): These are the sequences of characters, namely words or sentences. E.g., country = "Japan"

2. Integers (int): These are the whole numbers, which can be both positive and negative. E.g., age = 42

3. Float (float): These are real numbers or numbers with a decimal point. E.g., pi = 3.14

4. Boolean (bool): These represent only True or False values. E.g.,

    # The following represents a True value

    is_tasty = True

    # The results of the following check whether the condition given is True or False

    print(2>1)

    print(2==1)

    print(2<1)

    # The output of the three print statements will be True, False, False, which represent a Boolean expression

5. List: Lists are a collection of things that are enclosed in square brackets separated by commas. E.g., last_ten_game_goals_Messi = [1,0,3,0,2,0,0,1] or shopping_list = ["tomato", "potato", "onion", "garlic"]

6. Tuple: These are similar to lists, but their values cannot be changed and are used to store multiple items in a single variable. Tuples are written using round brackets. E.g.,

    # The following tuple stores a person's information (name, age)

person_info = ("Tom", 35)

7. Dictionary: Dictionaries are a collection of key–value pairs that help associate a meaning to each value in a collection of values. These can be created by placing a sequence of elements within curly brackets with a colon separating each key from its associated value. E.g.,

Store_locations = {"headquarters": "New York", "flagship": "Paris", "branch": "London"}

8. Set: Sets are the fourth and final built-in data types in Python. The other three have been covered in bullets 5 through 7. Sets are used to store unordered, unindexed, and unchangeable (although items can be added and removed) items in a single variable.[xx][xxi] E.g.,

Tom_fruits = {"apple", "mango", "orange", "kiwi"}

Python Constant

Python also has constants, which are a type of variable that holds unchangeable values. These constants are typically referenced from other files. Imagine constants as the wheels of a car. While one can customize their car in any way from the color (if you are super rich and want to purchase a Rolls Royce, you have forty-four thousand color combinations to choose from) to its emblem and wheel styles, the cars will always have wheels or tires (unless you are from the future where cars have started hovering!) making them a constant.

Using constants is a way to protect programmers from accidentally changing their values in the code (this feature might have been added keeping in mind coders who don't sleep at night). Constants make codes more readable and maintainable.

The value associated with a specific constant can be of any data type, just like with variables. Therefore, you can specify integer constants, float constants, characters constants, string constants, and more.

Python does not contain any predefined constants. Nor does it have a dedicated syntax for defining constants. As a result, to have a constant in Python, you must declare a variable but never change it. Now, the question coming to your mind should be how does anyone know whether a given variable is a constant?

This is where the naming convention comes into the picture. As mentioned above, there is nothing defined by Python on how the constants should be named, but the Python community has broadly agreed on using a strong naming convention to distinguish the two. Users should ideally create constants using the following rules:

- Constants should be named using uppercase. E.g.,
    - PI = 3.14 # *The value of pi*
    - SPEED_OF_LIGHT_KM_PER_SECOND = 300000 # *This means light can go around the Earth in .13 seconds. Imagine that. In the time you read that, light just went around the earth fifteen times.*
    - MAX_PASSWORD_ATTEMPTS = 3 # *This constant helps control how many times a user can attempt to enter their password before being locked out.*
- Constants should not begin with digits, except for underscore.

- No other special character (#,@,$,^) is utilized when declaring a constant.[xxii]

Python Variable Types: Local and Global[xxiii]

Local and Global, sounds interesting right? While these might not be as interesting as traveling the globe and trying what the locals eat, within the context of Python, these are very useful. Let's take a closer look at what they mean.

Global Variables: Variables that are declared outside of the function are known as global variables. We can access global variables inside or outside the function. A global variable declared outside the function can also be used inside a function as long as there is no other variable with a similar name inside.

Local Variables: Variables that are declared inside the function's body are known as local variables. These cannot be used outside the function.

Here is an example of how a global variable works:

global_variable = 100
print(global_variable)
 # This will give the output 100

```python
def understanding_global():
    print(global_variable)
```
 # This is defining a function that will print the value of global_variable when the function is called

```
understanding_global()
```

 # The function is called here, and it will give the output 100 even though the global_variable is defined outside the function

#The output for the above code will be

100

100

Now let's try to understand how a local variable works using a simple example:

```python
global_variable = 100
print(global_variable)
# This will give the output 100

def understanding_local():
    local_variable = 200
    print(local_variable)
```
 # This is defining a function that will print the value of local_variable when the function is called

```
understanding_local()
```

 # The function is called here, and it will give the output 200 because the local_variable is defined inside the function

print(local_variable)

 # This tries to print the value of local_variable, but it will result in an error because local_variable is defined inside a function, but we are trying to print it outside the function. We will get the error: NameError: name 'local_variable' is not defined.

How to Delete a Variable?

Variables can be deleted using the command "del" followed by the variable name. Once a variable is deleted, it can no longer be accessed. Upon trying to access a deleted variable, the following error message will be shown: *NameError: name 'variable_name' is not defined.*

Here is a simple example:

variable_to_be_deleted = "Delete me"
print(variable_to_be_deleted)
 # This will print "Delete me"

del variable_to_be_deleted
 # This will delete the variable

print(variable_to_be_deleted)

 # Trying to print this variable now will lead to an error: NameError: name "variable_to_be_deleted" is not defined.

Just to reiterate, Python reads the code line by line and gives the output accordingly. Therefore, in the example above, "Delete me" will be output once, which will be followed by the error because the variable has now been deleted.

4. Control Flow and Conditionals

We have several choices to make in our lives. Based on the information, we may decide to do one thing or another. For example, you could stream the world's content on your laptop screen, but you are choosing to learn and upskill instead. This choice helps you move in the direction you choose.

Similarly, when you code, you need your program to do one thing or another depending on the different options available. For example, if the password is correct, the user can log in. If it isn't correct, they get an error message to type the password again.

Programming is done to simplify certain tasks. Working on scenarios that simulate real-world choices is crucial in problem-solving. We use statements with certain conditions based on the requirements in programming languages. To do this in Python, we use certain statements (if/else/elif). These statements help the program make choices based on the conditions we specify.

In Python, control flow refers to the way program statements or blocks of codes are executed or assessed. It determines the order in which we execute the code, allowing for different paths or actions based on specific conditions.

Control flow in Python is regulated by conditional statements (if, else, and elif), loops/iterative statements (for and while), and branching/transfer statements (break, continue, and pass) to control the flow and execution of the program.

Before we code these, let's first try to understand these useful statements that will form the core of any coding you do.

Conditional Statements[xxiv]

If statement:

We use conditional statements to return whether a given comparison between two variables is True or False. Statements are used in combination with "if," "if else," and "else if" statements. For a single condition, we use "if," for double "if else," and for multiple conditions, we use "else if." For example, if the weather is nice, then I will go out and play football, else I will sit at home and watch television. The if statement in Python determines one can perform this sort of decision-making. It allows for conditional implementation of a statement or group of statements based on the value of an expression.

Before we get into this further, it is important to know what conditional operators are. Conditional operators are like the traffic rules. If you are crossing a road without understanding the road signs, you might cause a lot of trouble. You could get hurt by moving traffic, and other folks on the road could also get confused by your actions.

Therefore, it is essential to learn about traffic operators and their functions. Similarly, we need to understand the conditional operators in Python, which will guide us to have a smoother flow of code without errors or unwanted results.

The conditional operators in Python include:

- == to test if two data types are equal to each other (A single = means a value is getting assigned. E.g., x = 2 gives x the value of 2, but x ==2 is checking whether x is equal to 2.)
- ! = to test if two data types are not equal to each other
- \> to test if one data type is greater than another
- < to test if one data type is less than another

- \>= to test if one data type is greater than or equal to another
- <= to test if one data type is less than or equal to another

Let's see how the example of the if statement works in Python. We will calculate the square of a number if it is greater than 6.

number = 8
if number > 6:
  #Calculate square
  print(number*number)

Output

64

If-else statement:

The conditional statement (if-else) examines the condition and executes the program when the condition is True. If the condition is false, it will execute the else or the remaining part of the block of code. Example:

w = 20
if w < 30:
  print('first set')
  print('w is small')
else:

```
print('second set')
print('w is large')
```

Output

```
first set
x is small
```

Using the same example but with a different value:

```
w = 40
if w < 30:
    print('first set')
    print('w is small')
else:
    print('second set')
    print('w is large')
```

Output

```
second set
w is large
```

In simple words, the above example is if w<30, then print "something," and if w is greater than 30, then print "something else."

Chain multiple if statement:

With the help of an elif statement (which stands for else if), we can check multiple conditions. The condition statement if-elif-else in Python has an elif block to chain multiple conditions one after another. This helps make complicated decisions by examining multiple conditions one by one, and if the condition is fulfilled, it executes the code. For example:

```python
math_marks = float(input("Enter your math marks: "))
# This asks the user to input information based on which the code will run. Also, the use of float here ensures that even decimal value will be accepted

if math_marks >= 90:
    grade = "A+"
elif math_marks >= 80:
    grade = "B+"
elif math_marks >= 70:
    grade = "C+"
elif math_marks >= 60:
    grade = "D+"
else:
    grade = "F"

print(f"Your math grade is: {grade}")
```

Output

Based on the marks entered, the output will be either A+ or B+ or C+ or D+ or F

Another important thing to note from this example is the use of the f-string. F-strings are generally used to inset variables into texts. In the example above, print(f"Your math grade is: {grade}"). Because we add "f" right before a string that contains the variable name in curly brackets { }, we will be able to use the value of the variable in the string itself. Here is another example for your reference.

name = "Anthony Gonsales"
age = 100

statement = f"My name is {name} and I am {age} years old."
print(statement)

Output
My name is Anthony Gonsales and I am 100 years old.

Loops (For and While)[xxv]

When we have a routine, we repeat certain daily actions and our life functions smoothly. We cook, drop off our kids at school, and (hopefully) exercise every day.

Similarly, in Python, we perform certain repeated tasks. For example, if we have to print all the natural numbers until one hundred, and if we start writing a print statement one by one, not only would the code be long and boring but also inefficient.

This is where loops play a crucial role and save a lot of time for a programmer. Loops are divided into two categories, *for* and *while* loops.

For Loops

A programmer would like to execute a group of numbers a specified number of times. *For* loops in Python are used when we want to repeat a sequence, such as a list, string, tuple, and other iterable items, a fixed number of times. *For* loops help with efficient repetition.

Say we want to calculate the total number of tickets sold for an artist's concert over the past decade.

 # The value of tickets sold is added as a list below

tickets_sold = [111000, 123456, 250134, 345800, 351500, 402000, 493500, 678697, 2020, 800200]

```
total_tickets = 0

for daily_tickets in tickets_sold:
    total_tickets += daily_tickets
# The for loop goes through the tickets_sold and adds each year's ticket sales to the total_tickets variable

print(f"Total tickets sold for the past decade: {total_tickets}")
```

Output

Total tickets sold for the past decade: 3558307

As you can see, the *for* function worked with a defined list of values (tickets_sold) and added them one by one to the total_tickets variable.

While Loops

While loops are a little different. They execute the program until a condition is true.

By using a *while* loop, we can ask the user to guess a lucky number or color until they get the correct answer, without knowing the number of attempts needed.

Sticking with the concert tickets example, let's say you want to create a program to manage ticket sales. Users should be able to purchase tickets only till they are available. Once the available tickets are sold out, the users should get a message that tickets are no longer available.

 # Define the total number of tickets available
tickets_available = 1000

 # Define a variable that keeps track of tickets sold
tickets_sold = 0

 # The loop below asks users to input the tickets required and, based on the remaining tickets, displays the relevant message
while tickets_available > 0:

 # The statement below asks users to input the number of tickets they want to buy. The use of 'int' means that only integers would be accepted as an input.
  tickets_to_buy = int(input("How many tickets do you want to buy? "))

 # In the if statement below, if the tickets required are more than 0 but less than the total tickets available, the tickets_sold variable gets added with the tickets bought, and the tickets_available variable gets subtracted with the tickets bought.

  if 0 < tickets_to_buy <= tickets_available:

   tickets_sold += tickets_to_buy
   tickets_available -= tickets_to_buy
   print(f"{tickets_to_buy} ticket(s) sold.")
 else:
   print("Tickets are no longer unavailable.") # If the if condition is not met, then a message gets displayed that tickets are no longer available

print("All tickets have been sold. Thank you!")

Branching (Break, Continue, and Pass)

In Python, there are three branching statements: break, continue, and pass. Sometimes the users want to change the normal flow of the program, which can be done using break, continue, and return conditions.

Break statement:[xxvi]

When the programmer wants to jump out of the loop function and resume the next statement in the program, they use the break statement. Believe it or not, there is almost a 100 percent chance that you would have used this functionality on your phone, without knowing the break statement was in play.

When you search for a particular contact on your phone, this is what is most likely happening behind the scenes. As soon as the system finds the relevant contact, it stops searching. While today's phones are a little more complex and they complete the search and show all relevant results, in this example, we'll keep things simpler.

Here is how a code like this would work.

```
# List of contacts
contact_list = ["Anna", "Bud", "Chow", "Dinesh", "Evelyn", "Fabio"]

# Input a name that needs to be searched
contact_name = input("Enter a name to search your contacts: ")

# At the beginning of the code, define a variable as False. If conditions are met, this variable will become True, ending the search
contact_found = False

# Search every contact in the list till a match is found
for contact in contact_list:
    if contact == contact_name:
        print(f"Contact '{contact_name}' found!")
        contact_found = True
        break
```

 # If the contact is not found, then a message is displayed
if contact_found == False:
　print(f"Contact '{contact_name}' not found.")

When a contact name that exists is entered, we get the message *"Contact 'name' found!"* In case the contact is not there, we get the message *"Contact 'name' not found!"*

As you may be able to tell, this is a very simplified version of the code. This example does not account for minor spelling mistakes and is case-sensitive (unless the case matches exactly, the right results will not be shown).

Adding these elements would mean more conditions being built, leading to longer codes. There are a few tools in Python, however, to make such things easier. What are these? Keep reading.

Continue statement:

This is used to end the running iteration in a *for* and *while* loop and continue with the next iteration. The loop function doesn't get terminated once we use the continue statement; it continues with the next iteration.

Can you guess where on your phones you might be using a similar functionality? Remember in the previous section we talked about how today's phones complete the search and show all relevant results. Well, a "continue" statement can help with that.[xxvii]

 # List of contacts
contacts = ["Anna", "Bud", "Chow", "Dinesh", "Evelyn", "Fabio"]

 # Input any letter of the name that needs to be searched
search_query = input("Enter any letter of the contact you need to search: ")

print("Search results:")
for contact in contacts:
    # Check if the search query is not in the contacts.
    if search_query.lower() not in contact.lower():
        continue # Skip contacts that don't match the search query

    print(contact)

In this case, if you search for the letter "o," you will get the following output because these names have the letter "o":

Search results:
Chow
Don
Fabio

How this differs from the "break" statement is that if you tried to enter "o" as the contact name in the "break" statement example, you would get the message *"Contact 'name' not found!"*

While the "break" and "continue" functionalities serve different purposes and work distinctly, they can get confusing. I get tripped by them now and then. It helps me to think of them in the following terms:

The "break" functionality exits the loop entirely when a condition is met. The "continue" functionality skips specific items in a loop but continues to go through all the items.

Also, a "break" statement will typically lead to a single outcome as the loop gets terminated. The "continue" statement can produce multiple outcomes as the loop continues to the next iteration.

With your eye for detail, you might have noticed the use of lower() in the example there. It is called a string method, which is a built-in Python function to transform a string to lowercase characters. This helps make the string comparison case insensitive.

Pass statement:[xxviii]

We use pass as a keyword when we want to emphasize a syntactically empty block. Pass statement triggers no action, nothing happens. An interpreter, coming across a pass statement, will return no operation.

Pass statements usually are used as placeholders or when handling exceptions.

The pass is the keyword In Python, which won't do anything. Sometimes there is a situation in programming where we need to define a syntactically empty block. We can define that block with the pass keyword.

days = ["Tuesday", "Friday", "Sunday"]
for day in days:
  pass
print(days)

Output
["Tuesday", "Friday", "Sunday"]

String Method[xxix]

There are many such useful, built-in functions, as shown in the table below.[xxx] Play around with these functions to see how they work.

It is interesting to note that the string methods always return new values. This means that the original string value remains unchanged.

Check out the following list from W3 Schools on the pages below.[xxxi]

You may notice that the examples are getting more complex. This has been done keeping in mind your enhanced understanding of Python. Therefore, I would like to congratulate you for staying the course and pushing through to continue your journey toward becoming a Python prodigy.

The examples are focused to incorporate things learned in the previous sections. Hopefully they fire up your neurons and solidify the connections that help you retain information and develop a better understanding.

Method	Description
capitalize()	Converts the first character to uppercase
casefold()	Converts a string into lowercase
center()	Returns a centered string
count()	Returns the number of times a specified value occurs in a string
encode()	Returns an encoded version of the string
endswith()	Returns True if the string ends with the specified value
expandtabs()	Sets the tab size of the string
find()	Searches the string for a specified value and returns the position of where it was found
format()	Formats specified values in a string
format_map()	Formats specified values in a string
index()	Searches the string for a specified value and returns the position of where it was found
isalnum()	Returns True if all characters in the string are alphanumeric
isalpha()	Returns True if all characters in the string are in the alphabet
isascii()	Returns True if all characters in the string are ASCII characters
isdecimal()	Returns True if all characters in the string are decimals
isdigit()	Returns True if all characters in the string are digits
isidentifier()	Returns True if the string is an identifier
islower()	Returns True if all characters in the string are lowercase
isnumeric()	Returns True if all characters in the string are numeric
isprintable()	Returns True if all characters in the string are printable
isspace()	Returns True if all characters in the string are whitespaces
istitle()	Returns True if the string follows the rules of a title

isupper()	Returns True if all characters in the string are uppercase
join()	Converts the elements of an iterable into a string
ljust()	Returns a left-justified version of the string
lower()	Converts a string into lowercase
lstrip()	Returns a left-trimmed version of the string
maketrans()	Returns a translation table to be used in translations
partition()	Returns a tuple where the string is parted into three parts
replace()	Returns a string where a specified value is replaced with a specified value
rfind()	Searches the string for a specified value and returns the last position of where it was found
rindex()	Searches the string for a specified value and returns the last position of where it was found
rjust()	Returns a right-justified version of the string
rpartition()	Returns a tuple where the string is parted into three parts
rsplit()	Splits the string at the specified separator and returns a list
rstrip()	Returns a right-trimmed version of the string
split()	Splits the string at the specified separator and returns a list
splitlines()	Splits the string at line breaks and returns a list
startswith()	Returns True if the string starts with the specified value
strip()	Returns a trimmed version of the string
swapcase()	Swaps cases; lowercase becomes uppercase, and vice versa
title()	Converts the first character of each word to uppercase
translate()	Returns a translated string
upper()	Converts a string into uppercase
zfill()	Fills the string with a specified number of 0 values at the beginning

5. Python Data Structure

Ever wondered why finding a book in a library is a lot easier than finding one on your bookshelf? Or finding tools for some handiwork or spices to cook up a storm in the kitchen is a lot easier at your home than someone else's?

Well, this is because libraries have everything indexed and categorized, whereas your bookshelf might be a bit more random. In your tool room or kitchen, you probably have stacked and stored everything based on what is easier for you to remember.

Similarly, Python uses data structures to organize, store, and categorize data efficiently. Data structures in Python determine the relationship between data and the operations that can be performed on it. They offer an efficient data management solution, freeing users to concentrate on solving complex problems.

Data structures are the fundamentals of almost all computer languages. And guess what? Python helps you learn these fundamentals in a simplified manner as compared to other languages. Different data structures make it easier to describe and access data, allowing more time to solve problems instead of searching for the right tools. Let's learn some theory. I promise it'll be short.

Abstract Data Type and Data Structures

Abstract data type (ADT) simplifies users' lives by focusing on essential information instead of full process or implementation. For example, when you work on your laptop or desktop, you might have ten different programs open. If you go into the task manager or an activity monitor application on a Mac, however, you will see there are hundreds of processes running in the background. We can't see what is going on at the backend and how things are running and operating, but as long as we can do what we want, we don't care, do we?

To take our toolbox example, each tool performs a function. We are only interested in what the tool does and how to use it, not how it was made. If we consider the simple task of taking a photo on a smartphone, even at a high level, we can expect around fifty-odd processes in the backend to provide a seamless user experience.

These processes include starting the camera app, using the physical camera, focusing, adjusting exposure, capturing the image, and saving it in the desired format. This still does not account for the processes that would be required to open the app itself.

Data structure: Implementing abstract data types (ADT) involves using data structure and requires assessing the actual data using a group of programming constructs and basic data types. Data structures can be compared to a bookshelf, storing books in an organized way. We divide data structures into two categories: primitive and non-primitive data structures.

Just a little more theory and we'll get into the interesting stuff.[xxxii]

Primitive and Non-primitive Data Structures[xxxiii]

You can compare the core difference between primitive and non-primitive data to the difference between books stored in the public library and books stored in your own house. They keep books in the public library in an organized way, with everything categorized and indexed. You won't find *Harry Potter and the Sorcerer's Stone* by J. K. Rowling in the same section as *War and Peace* by Leo Tolstoy. Thank God for that, or Mr. Tolstoy would turn in his grave.

Books at your home might be randomly kept or might follow a categorization that only makes sense to you, like, by color or thickness (hopefully not).

Both types of data structures are important in Python. They are essential for organizing and manipulating data effectively.

Primitive data structures are essential building blocks that represent basic data structures. Regardless of your work, you must organize, store, and change data to meet your needs.

Primitive data structures, also called "fundamental" or "built-in" data types, store data of one particular type. They are directly operated by machine instructions. They always have a value and are of a fixed size.

There are four types of primitive data variables:

- **Integers:** Integers are used to represent numeric data, especially whole numbers. For example. 0, 1, 2, -1, 200, etc. are integers. These are the whole numbers, which can be both positive and negative.

  If you want the user to enter the number of students in a class, you want to ensure only integer values are input, unless you have watched too much *Two and a Half Men*.

- **Float:** This is used to store real numbers having decimal points. Numbers like 3.14, 0.11, etc. are all such examples.

  If your application requires someone to enter their weight, it would be useful to capture it as a float for more accuracy. Not doing so has had comical tragedies as well as disastrous consequences. NASA's Mariner 1 spacecraft, designed to fly by Venus and collect data, had to be destroyed right after takeoff because its horizontal velocity was calculated incorrectly because of a rounding error, leading to a loss of around 160 million dollars. Imagine that.[xxxiv]

- **Strings:** These are the sequences of characters, namely words or sentences. We add values in enclosed quotes, either in single, double, or triple quotes. For example, 'Africa', "Middle East", '''Europe''' are strings.

- **Boolean:** Booleans evaluate the expressions and represent the True value of an expression (True or False). These are used in conditional and comparisons.

Example:

a = 1
b = 1
print(a == b)

Outcome
True

```
a = 1
b = 2
print(a == b)
```

Outcome
False

NoneType (None): Represents the absence of a value or a null value.

Non-Primitive Data Structures[xxxv]

Non-primitive data structures can store more than one data type. For example, we can add a string as well as an integer in a list. They are derived from primitive data types and can have void/null values. Non-primitive data structures start with an uppercase character. These are further categorized as follows:

Lists: In Python, lists are a very important data type. When you have several items that you need to store as a single unit, you can make a list for that. For example, you can have a list of planets that will look like [Mercury, Venus, Earth, Mars, Jupiter, Saturn, Uranus, Neptune]. (No hard feelings, Pluto.)

There are some key features lists have that differentiate them from other data structures.

1. Lists are ordered. This is useful if you want to access a particular item in the list. You can do so by accessing its position or index in the list. Remember, the index starts at 0. Each item in a specified list has its unique index value.
For example:

["Mercury", "Venus", "Earth", "Mars", "Jupiter", "Saturn", "Uranus", "Neptune"]
   [0]   [1]   [2]   [3]   [4]   [5]   [6]   [7]

Mercury is the first planet, but its index is [0]. Venus is the second planet with its position being [1], followed by Earth, which is at position [2], and so on. If you write an index eight, you will get an error, as there is no value in the code.

Negative indexing will have values from the list, but from the end of the list—i.e., the last item has index [-1], second to last item [-2], and third to last item [-3].

2. Lists are mutable. You can make changes to a list. For example, you can add, remove, or modify items. This is useful in cases where data gets updated. For example, if a new student gets added to a classroom, the list can

be modified accordingly. You can use methods like append() and pop() to add or remove elements. If we add new items to the existing list, the new ones will be placed at the end of the list.

3. Lists are heterogeneous. You can have different data types within a single list. For example:
roger_stats = ["Roger Federer", 185, 85, 20, 81.97]. The list gives the name (string), height in cm (integer), weight in kg (integer), number of grand slams won (integer), and career win percentage (float).

4. Lists can be sliced. We talked about how lists can be indexed. For example, if we want to access Roger Federer's grand slams won, we would use roger_stats[3]. If we want to access his statistics, like name, height, and weight, we can use roger_stats[0:3], which gives us the output: *['Roger Federer', 185, 85]*.

5. Lists have inbuilt operations like sort(), which sorts the list in ascending order, or reverse(), which reverses the order of the list. You can also nest lists. For example, nested_list = [[Apple, Banana], [Potatoes, Onions]]

6. Lists can have duplicate values, and items in a list are separated by commas and enclosed within square brackets.

7. Generally, the order of the items cannot be changed. (There are ways to change the order, but they are outside the scope of this book.)

Tuples: Just like lists, tuples are also sequencing data types. Tuples are an ordered collection of data elements and store multiple elements in a single variable. Like lists, items in a tuple are separated by commas but are enclosed within round brackets.

Overall, tuples are quite similar to lists, but there is one major difference: You cannot alter or change tuple values. In other words, tuples are immutable. This means once you assign the value in a tuple, you cannot delete or alter any value inside it. This feature is useful in cases where we do not want the items to change.[xxxvi]

For example, a school maintains a list of their students, student IDs, and average grades of the past three years. In this case, the tuple would look something like this:

all_students = (('John Doe', '11223344', [95, 92, 91]), ('Anna Chow', '22334455', [56, 67, 62]), ('Dinesh Singh', '33445566', [79, 83, 75]))

You would probably not want this information to be changed even by mistake. Therefore, using tuples here would be ideal.

Other features, such as the order of the items, heterogeneity, indexing, and slicing, remain the same as lists.[xxxvii]

Dictionary: We all have dictionaries in our houses. Maybe some still use them, but if you're like me, you probably Google the meaning every time you come across a new word.

When using a traditional physical dictionary, we look for a word and then its meaning. For example, if I look up the word "Python" in the *Oxford Dictionary*, one of the definitions we see is the following:

Python, n.[1] —Any of various large, heavy-bodied, non-venomous snakes constituting the family Pythonidae, found in tropical parts of Africa, Asia, and Australasia . . .[xxxviii]

For some reason, I was hoping Python, the programming language, would be the first result, but it was not meant to be.

In this example, "python" the word can be considered the "key," while its meaning could be the "value." Together, this forms a key–value pair. You must be wondering why convolute this, but in the context of Python, the programming language, this is an important concept.

In Python, dictionaries have key–value pairs, where each key has a specific value. This helps establish a relation between items. For example:

student_id = {"John Doe":"11223344", "Anna Chow": "22334455", "Dinesh Singh": "33445566"}

The names are the keys, whereas the IDs are the values.

You must be wondering why this is useful and why not just use a list. And you could, but dictionaries just make it easier. If you wanted a student's ID, you could simply use the following and get the desired result:

id = student_id["John Doe"]

This will give you the output: *11223344*.

Like lists, the values are mutable. The keys, however, are unique. In case you attempt to add a duplicate key, the new value will overwrite the older one. This ensures that each key has only one associated value. Dictionaries are also useful for categorization and grouping. For example, you could group movies by genre or students by their grades.

In terms of syntax, dictionary elements are the key–value pairs that are separated by commas and enclosed within curly brackets { }.[xxxix]

Sets: A set is a collection of distinct, unique, and well-defined items. In case you don't want your data set to have duplicates, using sets is the way to go. Sets are placed using curly brackets. Also, you can change data entries once inserted into the program.

For example, if you want to create a list of people whose initials start with the letter "A," you collect the data from different individuals. It's likely you'd encounter some repetitions. Using sets will ensure unique values remain in the data set. You can also use this feature to remove duplicates from a list.

usernames = {"user1", "user2", "user4", "user3", "user1", "user2"}
unique_usernames = set(usernames)
print(unique_usernames)

Output: {'user1', 'user2', 'user3', 'user4'} # Duplicates removed

Another interesting feature of sets is that they are an unordered collection of data elements (unlike tuples, dictionaries, or lists). So, when you try to print a set, the order of the items will change randomly. For example:

Feature	Lists	Sets	Dictionaries	Tuples
Ordered	Yes (Maintain order)	No (Unordered)	No (Unordered)	Yes (Maintain order)
Mutable	Yes (Can be modified)	Yes (Can be modified)	Yes (Can be modified)	No (Immutable)
Allows Duplicates	Yes (Duplicate values)	No (Unique values)	No (Unique keys)	Yes (Duplicate values)
Brackets	Square brackets [ ]	Curly brackets { }	Curly brackets { }	Round brackets ( )
Access by Index	Yes (e.g., my_list[0])	No	No (By key, e.g., my_dict['key'])	Yes (e.g., my_tuple[0])
Common Use Cases	Where sequences or dynamic data is required	Where unique values are required	Where mapping, key–value pairs are required	Where fixed sequences or immutable data is required

random_set = {"Roger Federer", 185, 85, 20, 81.97}
print(random_set)

The output for this came out to be {81.97, 20, 85, 185, 'Roger Federer'} on the first try and then {'Roger Federer', 81.97, 20, 85, 185} on the second try.

Aren't these data structures interesting? Before you get confused between these different data structures, the following table shows a snapshot of the similarities and differences for your reference.[xl]

As you get more comfortable with these concepts, you'll see the numerous functionalities these data structures provide. A few simple ones can be found below.

Concatenation (+): Two variables, x and y, with the string values "chocolate" and "cake," respectively, can be brought together using the "+" operator.

x = "chocolate"
y = "cake"
print(x + " " + "&" + " " + y) # Notice the use of extra spaces by using " "

Output: chocolate and cake

This can be used for lists as well –

list_1 = ["we", "will"]

list_2 = ["rock", "you"]
combined_list = list_1 + list_2
print(combined_list)

Output: *['we', 'will', 'rock', 'you']*

(*) We can use the multiplication operator to repeat a string a certain number of times.

x = "chocolate"
repeat_x = x*3
print(repeat_x)

Output: *chocolatechocolatechocolate*

list_1 = ["we", "will"]
list_2 = ["rock", "you"]
repeat_list = list_1 * 3
print(repeat_list)

Output: *['we', 'will', 'we', 'will', 'we', 'will']*

Length (len): We can identify the length of a string, lists, tuples, sets, and dictionaries using the len() operator.

names = "Chocolate,cake" *# String example*
print(len(names))
Output: *14*

student_id = {"John Doe":"11223344", "Anna Chow": "22334455", "Dinesh Singh": "33445566" } # Dictionary example
print(len(student_id))
Output: 3

planets = ["Mercury", "Venus", "Earth", "Mars", "Jupiter", "Saturn", "Uranus", "Neptune"] # *List example*
print(len(planets))
Output: 8

in: What if we want to check whether an item is present in the list, set, tuple, or dictionary? We can do this by using the "in" operator.

fruits = ["Apple", "Banana", "Oranges"]
if "Apple" in fruits:
    print("Apple is present.")
else:
    print("Apple is absent.")
Output: Apple is present

Union, difference, intersection: These three are used to perform operations between sets.

- The union operator "|" returns a set with only the unique values from multiple sets.

- The difference operator "-" returns the set of elements that are present in the first set but not in the second one.
- The intersection operator "&" showcases elements that are common in both sets.

set1 = {1, 2, 3}
set2 = {3, 4, 5}
union = set1 | set2   # Union
difference = set1 - set2   # Difference
intersection = set1 & set2   # Intersection

 # Another way to code these is:

union = set1.union(set2) # Union
intersection = set1.intersection(set2) # Difference
difference = set1.difference(set2) # Intersection

print(union)
print(intersection)
print(difference)

 # The result in both cases will be the same

Output: {1, 2, 3, 4, 5}

Output: {3}

Output: {1, 2}

This brings us to the end of this chapter. Give yourself a pat on the back. You deserve it.

6. Python Functions

Recall how WhatsApp used to work when it was newly launched and how it has developed since then? From teenagers using it to chat with their friends, it has evolved into a product that enables businesses to conduct their operations. Fifty million companies around the world use WhatsApp as a marketing channel.[xli] That is quite something.

For instance, a homemaker used to send individual messages for their business, but now they use the broadcast feature to reach everyone at once. For better or worse, this changed the game for everyone. It reduced the repetitive and mundane tasks and created a function that could repeat "n" number of tasks at the click of a button.

This is exactly what functions in Python do. (You didn't see that coming now, did you?)

Yes, Python allows you to create functions that can perform tasks without the need to code again and again. You can create functions in Python as blocks of code that perform specific tasks and can be reused multiple times. They group commonly or repeatedly executed tasks together, allowing for code readability and reusability. By using functions, we can avoid repeatedly writing the same code for different inputs.

Think of Python functions as pizza bases. If you go to your closest pizza store, they might have dozens of pizza types with different toppings. But the base remains the same. Most times, they would simply pull out a prepared base, put in the desired toppings, and give the pizza a fancy-sounding name. Not that anyone cares because pizzas are delicious! Using the same analogy, we can convert lengthy codes into functions, which can save a lot of time and effort. And when we want to use it, we call it and use it.

There are two types of functions in Python: built-in library functions and user-defined functions. Let's look at each.

Built-in library function: Thank God we have a built-in library in Python; otherwise my decision to learn Python further would have taken a U-turn from here. The built-in library will save a lot of time for coders, and more so for beginners. These pre-defined codes are like small shortcuts that can save you from writing codes every time you have to access them.

Functions that are defined and pre-coded in Python are called built-in library functions. Some examples of built-in library functions are min(), max(), len(), sum(), range(), dict(), list(), tuple(), set(), type(), print(), etc.[xlii]

We have gone through all these, and now that you think about it, there are indeed functions. The reason for writing max() gives you the max is because somewhere in the backend someone defined this function. Therefore, when I write the following, I get an answer right away.

Print(max(1,2,3,4,5))

Output: 5

If it weren't for this built-in function, you would have to use *for* loops, if statements, and whatnot just to perform a simple task like finding the maximum.

Now, imagine you wanted to count the letters of one of the longest words in the dictionary—"Hippopotomonstrosesquippedaliophobia." I am not making this up. It is an actual word, and you won't believe it when I tell you what it means. It means the fear of long words.

Anyway, back to the topic. To calculate the length of this word, there is another built-in function in Python called len(). As you can imagine, it calculates the length, and here is how it can be used.

Longest_word =
"Hippopotomonstrosesquippedaliophobia"
print(len(longest_word))

Output: 36

That was easy, wasn't it?

Similarly, the other built-in functions also ease writing code in Python. They are listed below for your convenience. As you become more comfortable with Python, you could start exploring these as well.

Built-In Functions[xliii]			
A abs() aiter() all() anext() any() ascii() **B** bin() bool() breakpoint() bytearray() bytes() **C** callable()	**E** enumerate() eval() exec() **F** filter() float() format() frozenset() **G** getattr() globals()	**L** len() list() locals() **M** map() max() memoryview() min() **N** next() **O** object()	**R** range() repr() reversed() round() **S** set() setattr() slice() sorted() staticmethod() str() sum() super()

Built-In Functions[xliii]			
chr() classmethod() compile() complex() **D** delattr() dict() dir() divmod()	**H** hasattr() hash() help() hex() **I** id() input() int() isinstance() issubclass() iter()	oct() open() ord() **P** pow() print() property()	**T** tuple() type() **V** vars() **Z** zip() __import__()

User-defined functions: Functions that are created by users to perform certain tasks as per requirement or need. Using the **def** keyword, Python allows us to create user-defined functions. We can add anything inside a function. The function identifier is followed by closed brackets and a colon. Let's take the following example, which does not use a function but performs a task.[xliv]

X = 2

y = 4
z = 6

avg = (x,y,z)/3
print (avg)

Output: 4.0

In the example above, we have calculated the average using a simple formula. If we had to calculate the average of another set of three numbers, we could write this out again and maybe a third time too. But, if there was a fourth one, we'd be out the door faster than the speed of light (remember from our earlier chapter?).

But if we use a function, it makes our lives easy, as you'll see below. We would convert this block of code into the function as follows:

def average(x,y,z):
   avg = (x+y+z)/3
   print (avg) # This completes our block of code and the function is defined

The job isn't done yet. While the function has been created, unless it is called, the function is of no use. Running the above block of code will not even give you an output. Here is what you need to do to call the function:

x = 2

y = 4
z = 6 .

average(x,y,z) # The function has been called here, and it uses the values shared above to automatically calculate the average

Output: 4.0

To make functions work, it is important to place arguments and parameters inside parentheses. For more clarity, let's discuss the difference between argument and parameter.

A parameter is the variable defined within the parentheses when we write or define a function (for example, x, y, and z in the example above are the parameters).

An argument is the value passed to a function; values 2, 4, and 6 are the arguments in the example above.

Just because we have a set of parameters in the parenthesis doesn't mean we can only use those. You could define a new set of parameters and call them in the function, and that would work too. Here is how:

whiskey = 40

tango = 50
foxtrot = 60

average(whiskey, tango, foxtrot)

Output: 50.0

Another way to call the function can be done simply as shown below:

average(10,20,30) # After a function has been defined, just calling the function with the values in it like this will also do the trick

Output: 20.0

Here is another simple example:

def greet(name):
 print(f"Hello, {name}! Good morning")

greet("Ana")
greet("Adam")

Output: Hello, Ana! Good morning

Hello, Elsa! Good morning

These examples are fairly simple. However, if you try to remember your days in high school (I can't as it seems it was a century ago), you might recall quadratic equations. The formula for that was this:

$$x = \frac{-b \pm \sqrt{b^2 - 4ac}}{2a}$$

Using functions for this formula is way better than typing it out manually every single time, don't you think? This is where functions can take multiple lines of code and perform the task through a simple line of code.

We briefly touched upon arguments in the section above. It is time for us to take a deeper dive into the different arguments. Don't worry, these arguments are unlike anything you probably see on the news or on "reality" shows.

In Python, when a function is called, parameters and arguments are used to pass information to the function, as discussed above. There are four types of arguments that one can provide in a function.

Default arguments provide a default value while creating a function. The function automatically assigns a default value if we provide no value within the function. We assign the default values to the argument by using "="—known as the assignment operator. We can define a function with many default arguments.[xlv]

For example,

def full_name(f_name, m_name, l_name):
    print("Hello,", f_name, m_name, l_name)

name("Ana", "Roy", "Mathew")

Outcome
Hello, Ana Roy Mathew

In the above example,
- full_name is the function name
- f_name, m_name, l_name are the parameters
- full_name("Ana", "Roy", "Mathew") is a function call
- "Ana", "Roy", and "Mathew" are the arguments.

Keyword argument: In Python, keyword arguments are when you assign values to arguments using their keyword names, followed by the variable name and "=" assignment operator. A keyword argument is also called a named argument. Here is how they work:

def doctor_details(name, age): # function with 2 keyword arguments print('Doctor Details:', name, age)

doctor_details('Jule', 45) # default function call

doctor_details(name='Ana', age=50) # Both keyword arguments are getting passed by explicitly naming the parameter along with its value

Outcome: Doctor Details: Jule 45

Doctor Details: Ana 50

Positional argument: These are the arguments that are passed to a function based on its order within the function's parameter list. We use these only when we know the order of the argument to be passed. The results will change if we change the order of the arguments. Order, hence, is the key aspect of positional argument. It is important to ensure that the horse is before the cart, not the other way around.[xlvi]

Def minus(x, y):
 return x − y

x, y = 50, 30
result1 = minus(y, x)
print("Used positional arguments:", result1)

 # We will get incorrect output because the expectation was (x–y) but we will get (y–x) because of the swapped position of values x and y

result2 = minus(x, y)
print("Used positional arguments:", result2)

Output:Used Positional arguments: –20

Used Positional arguments: 20

Variable length argument: Python functions can accept a variable number of arguments as well. This feature is useful when the programmer doesn't know the number of arguments beforehand. There are two types of arguments—arbitrary positional and arbitrary keyword. To pass them, use "*" or "**" before the argument names. For example, def name(*students) or def name(**students). The first example can have any number of students in the argument. The second is keyword-specific and allows for any number of key–value pairs to be passed as arguments.[xlvii]

7. Input and Output Operations

One area where Python provides further support is file handling. This section covers file-handling functions, including opening, closing, creating, writing, reading, and updating files.

The way we store our files in the new folder or any folder of your choice on the desktop and access these files anytime we want. This is what Python does, too, when handling files. We open a new file, write our content in it, and save it in the folder. We can re-write it and update these files whenever we want to and then close it.

File-handling functions are essential for managing files in Python. They include creating a file, writing data into a file, reading data from a file, and updating the contents of a file. These functions enable users to interact with files and store information generated by programs.

The main purpose of the file handling is to manage the data efficiently. Python allows users to create different files that can store and manipulate data for the programs.

We classify files in Python into two types: normal text files and binary files. Text files contain lines of text, with each line terminated by a special character. Binary files store data using binary language composed of zeros and ones and do not require line terminators. To make the data understandable to machines, it is converted into binary format before being stored in the file.[xlviii]

Normal text files: The text files in Python store data in ASCII or UNICODE format. These two are the most extensively used character encoding standards. The UNICODE format is known as the universal character encoding used primarily to process, store, and enable the interchange of text data in any language. We use ASCII for the illustration of text, such as letters, digits, symbols, etc., in computers.

Each character occupies one byte of space. For example, "123.33" will occupy six bytes of space as if we count the number of characters. Each line is finished by an EOL (end of a line) character, which is "\n" (escape character, this adds new lines, this comes automatically in the file) or "\r."

Python provides different modes for accessing files. These modes determine the specific operations that can be performed on the files.

Multiple modes to open a file in Python:[xlix]

Mode	Description
'r'	Opens a file for reading, and by default, it opens in the reading mode
'r+'	Opens a file for reading and then writing
'w'	Opens a file for writing. We create a file first if there is no file, or truncate it if there is any file
'w+'	Opens for writing and then reading. This mode may overwrite the existing data
'a'	Opens a file for appending
'a+'	Opens for appending and then reading. This mode will not overwrite the existing data
'b'	Opens a file in the binary mode
'x'	Opens a file for the exclusive creation
't'	Opens a file in the text mode
'+'	Opens a file for updating (reading and writing)

Opening a File: Just as you would with any other file on your computer, you first open it and then work on it. You start by going to the folder where the file resides and then open it. Python follows the same process. It provides an open() function to open a file. When you open a file, there are three things required—the name of the file, its location, and what you want to do with the file or the mode of the file. In Python, the mode will be "r" for reading, "w" for writing, and "a" for appending. We'll cover all these below.

As always, let's start with an example. But to make it interesting, the file we are going to access contains lyrics to one of Taylor Swift's top songs—"Shake It Off." So, let's shake it off . . . I mean . . . Let's get started!

 # Example file path on a Windows system. Please note that this code will not run in your system unless your computer name is a mirror image of mine . . . which would be scary, actually!

file_location =
"C:\\Users\\xxxx\\OneDrive\\Desktop\\Shake It Off - Taylor Swift.txt"
taylor_swift_lyrics = open(file_location,"r")

 # The code above has opened the file in Python

Do note that the file has opened in read mode. This means all Python can do right now is read the file and not write or append the file).

With this code, we won't see anything in the output yet because we haven't asked Python to do anything with the open file.

Another thing to note here is that backslashes (\) are used in Windows file paths to divide folders. A single backslash is an escape character in Python strings, so if you use a backslash in a string, you must use a double backslash (\\).[1]

Reading files: Once we open the file we need to read its content. For this we use the read() method.

first_line = taylor_swift_lyrics.readline()
print(first_line)

 # The code above prints the first line of the file. In my case, the first list is the name of the song, so the output is: "Shake It Off"

all_lines = taylor_swift_lyrics.readlines()
print(all_lines)

 # The code above prints all the lines of the file. So, I won't reproduce the output here as it will contain the entire song lyrics (all 584 words)

content = taylor_swift_lyrics.read()
print(content)

 # The code above also prints all the lines in the file, but it prints it with line breaks

Writing files: Let's say you felt creative and thought you could enhance the lyrics of the song in some way. If this is the case, as much as I don't want you to, I would strongly suggest putting Python on the back burner and pursuing a different career. Or use that creativity to write the most beautiful code the world has ever seen.

If you want to write to a file, there are two ways. You could write to a file, and you could append to a file. Writing to a file replaces the existing content with your new content, whereas appending to a file preserves the existing content and adds the new content to the file.

taylor_swift_lyrics = open(file_location,"w") # This opens the file to write
taylor_swift_lyrics.write("Don't Shake It Off") # This will replace the existing content

taylor_swift_lyrics = open(file_location,"a") # This opens the file to append
taylor_swift_lyrics.write("Don't Shake It Off") # This will add to the existing content

Closing file: Once we have written our content in the file, we cannot simply leave the file as it is. Like everyone, Python needs proper closure to avoid any lingering "feelings." But unlike real life, Python is well equipped to get closure quickly, as you'll see in the example below. It's important because it saves the file.[li]

taylor_swift_lyrics.close # This closes the file

Binary files: Normal text files are great for storing the lyrics of Taylor Swift's songs. But, what if you wanted to open the videos of one of the songs? This is where binary files come in. Binary files store data in the same format as stored in the memory. Binary files are not readable by the users, as they are in the binary format that is 0 and 1. We can read binary files by using file mode and the "read" method.[lii]

In Python, binary files can be read or written using modes like "rb," or read binary, and "wb," or write binary.

Let's touch upon a very useful part of Python. Input and output functions. We'll start with something you already know:

Output functions (print function): Programmers who want to print the output can use the built-in function print(). You've seen this in all our examples, so you probably know this like the back of your hand.

Input functions: Imagine talking to someone and them saying something that really hits home. That feels good, right? Maybe that's why people, including me, like video games so much. They respond to your inputs immediately, which gives you a good feeling, and probably that's what makes them so addictive.[liii]

You can provide inputs in the Python program by using the input() function similar to video games. These inputs can be used by the program to perform tasks as per your commands, like Aladdin's genie. Well, maybe not that cool, but you get the idea. The input function returns values as strings or characters, hence you pass that into a variable. For example:

name = input()

print("The name is:", name)

In the above example, we have created a basic program to take the "input." As soon as you run the program, you will see a blank screen waiting for your input. Once you enter the input, you'll see it get printed on the screen, followed by the print statement like below:

Bond, James Bond

The name is: Bond, James Bond

A more efficient way of doing this is:

Name = input("The name is: ")

In this case, once the program is running, you will be prompted with "The name is: " followed by an opportunity to enter the name. So, essentially you will see:

The name is: Bond, James Bond

From the above examples, we can see that the "input" function assigns strings to the variable, which the user inputs. Whatever we add as input in "name" will be stored as a string. So even if you enter a number, Python's input function cannot detect your number. Instead, it will treat your input as a string. For example:

b = input("Enter your first number: ")
c = input("Enter your second number: ")
print(b+c)

Output: Enter your first number: 10

Enter your second number: 20

1020

So, adding b and c will not give us the result of 30, but instead, it will give us 1020. But don't worry, there is an easy way to fix this. We do this by letting Python know what type of value we are entering.

If we want an arithmetic operation, we do it only if both the inputs are integers using the syntax "int":

```
b = input("Enter your first number: ")
c = input("Enter your second number: ")
print(int(b) + int(c))
```

Output: Enter your first number: 10

Enter your second number: 20

30

What if we have a "float"?

```
b = input("Enter your first number: ")
c = input("Enter your second number: ")
print(int(b) + int(c))
```

Output: Enter your first number: 10

Enter your second number: 20

30.0 #Notice the decimal followed by 0 as an indication that the result is a float

8. Modular Programming

The name may sound scary, but it simply refers to breaking down a complex system into smaller components or modules that can be created, tested, and used independently. Modular design has been widely used in engineering even before computers existed. Nowadays, almost every product, such as cars and mobile phones, heavily relies on modularization.

What Are Modules?[liv]

Did you ever borrow a pen from your classmate, or a book from your friend? If you have, essentially, you have used a module. Modules are the group of functions, variables, and classes that are saved in Python.

Described simply, modules are used to borrow someone else's code. Imagine you had to create a program that downloaded your favorite comics, organized them in files, and saved them in designated folders. Now picture yourself finding someone who had developed a code to download comics but was limited only to that. You could use that code as a module since it is tried and tested and will save you a lot of time.

If I like to eat pasta in the middle of the night and I already have a prepared pasta sauce, I could make a Michelin-star dish in a few minutes. Similarly, modules provide you the flexibility to use files saved in Python and use it for new programs. They help programmers break large complex compilations of codes into separate, manageable elements. We can then collect each module and build a larger program or an application.

A Python module is any file with the .py extension that contains valid Python code. There is no specific syntax required to define a module. After importing a module, we can access its objects. We can retrieve these objects after an import command. There are many alternatives to importing a module. If I have to create a new project and can optimize my time by using already created and saved files, I will use the module function for this purpose. Importing files allows for code reusability.

Types of Modules

The concept is like pre-cooked and fresh-cooked food. While everyone likes to eat freshly cooked food, which involves effort and time, sometimes people defer to eating pre-cooked. Similarly, modules are of two types that are predefined and user-defined.

Pre-defined modules are those modules that are already defined by the users like, 'random," "calendar," "keyword," etc., and these modules are already stored in Python.

Both types of modules will perform the same function—that is, re-use of codes. The pre-defined module will have pre-defined developed codes that can directly be imported and used.[lv]

Here is a simple example of importing "Calendar":

import calendar
print(calendar.month(2034,1)) *# If you are curious as to why I chose the year 2034 to showcase, well, that's because year 2034 will follow the same calendar as year 2023.*

Output:

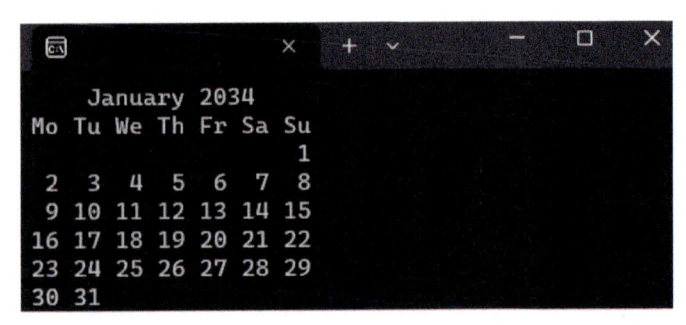

```
    January 2034
Mo Tu We Th Fr Sa Su
                   1
 2  3  4  5  6  7  8
 9 10 11 12 13 14 15
16 17 18 19 20 21 22
23 24 25 26 27 28 29
30 31
```

By importing "Calendar," we are able to use it. Imagine if we had to create a calendar in Python. It would be several lines of code so using the pre-defined calendar module is certainly easier.

User-defined modules are created by a user without using any pre-defined module. And the way you're progressing, soon you will be creating your modules. Before you do that, though, you'll be happy to know that there are already around two hundred modules stored within the standard library of Python.[lvi] You can import these modules as and when required based on your needs.

For example,

 # Import standard math module
import math

 # use math.pi to get value of pi
print("The value of pi is", math.pi)

Output: The value of pi is 3.141592653589793

Designing and writing modules: Modules are simplified versions of complex files, lines, and codes. They store Python definitions and statements all in a single file. We provide names to modules by removing the suffix ".py." Also, we can rename the importing module. In the example below, we will rename math.pi to MP.pi:

 # Import module by renaming it

import math as MP

print(MP.pi)

Outcome: 3.141592653589793

Above, we have renamed the math module as MP and we see that we get the desired result.

We can also import precise names from a module without importing the entire module. For example, we can import only pi from the math module from the above example.

from math import pi
print (pi)

Outcome: 3.1415926535897930

dir() built-in function: the dir() is a built-in function. If the user wants to list down all the characteristics and methods of any particular module, they can use the built-in function dir() with the name of the module as an argument. This function will return a list of defined names in a namespace. If you try to do it without an argument, the following is what you will get.

 # without importing any module

print(dir())

Output:

['__annotations__', '__builtins__', '__cached__', '__doc__', '__file__', '__loader__', '__name__', '__package__', '__spec__']

If you try to do it with math, you will see several mathematical functions that you probably last saw in high school.

print(dir(math))

Output

['__doc__', '__loader__', '__name__', '__package__', '__spec__', 'acos', 'acosh', 'asin', 'asinh', 'atan', 'atan2', 'atanh', 'cbrt', 'ceil', 'comb', 'copysign', 'cos', 'cosh', 'degrees', 'dist', 'e', 'erf', 'erfc', 'exp', 'exp2', 'expm1', 'fabs', 'factorial', 'floor', 'fmod', 'frexp', 'fsum', 'gamma', 'gcd',

'hypot', 'inf', 'isclose', 'isfinite', 'isinf', 'isnan', 'isqrt', 'lcm', 'ldexp', 'lgamma', 'log', 'log10', 'log1p', 'log2', 'modf', 'nan', 'nextafter', 'perm', 'pi', 'pow', 'prod', 'radians', 'remainder', 'sin', 'sinh', 'sqrt', 'tan', 'tanh', 'tau', 'trunc', 'ulp']

Module search path: When we import modules it is possible to trace its location. As soon as the programmer executes the import statement, it will search for the .py file in a list of directories assembled from multiple sources. It can identify the current directory from which the script was run, or from the list of directories that are in the PYTHONPATH environment variables.

Packages: Once we have created multiple modules, we may lose their count and respective roles. It is best to organize the modules in a compendium or package. A package is a collection of related modules, and one could consider a library as a collection of packages. The "pip" command is used to install these packages. It allows the user to install and manage packages that aren't part of the two hundred standard modules discussed above.

You can download these packages and libraries and use them in your programs. Whatever module you want to use or want to install for your program, it would be available on the internet. There are multiple such packages and libraries available.

One example is sklearn. Sklearn is considered to be the most useful library for machine learning in Python. Its use cases would include fraud detection (by identifying anomalies based on historical data), image classification (automatic grouping of photos on the phone), etc.[lvii]

The potential in Python is endless. On that note, why don't we create a few small projects in the final chapter of this book?

9. Small Python Projects

Look at us! How far we have come! From novices to almost experts. Since we've learned the basics of Python, let's create some code to solve real-life problems, like rock-paper-scissors.

This is one global problem that needs solving. Don't know about you, but these games have reliably resolved many of my problems, like who sat in the front seat or who got to open the packet of chips. I think this could also solve most global disputes, but nobody listens to me about this. Oh well, their loss!

On a more serious note, we will, in this chapter, showcase what we have achieved so far in Python through three projects. We will create codes and functions and show how Python can solve real-life problems. These projects allow you to explore Python's capabilities and learn creatively. The projects include a simple calculator, a mad libs game, and a rock-paper-scissors game.

The calculator uses variables, operators, and functions to do math and solve equations. Mad Libs uses string manipulation to ask for words and create fun stories. The rock-paper-scissors game uses interaction, random numbers, and conditional statements to simulate and decide the winner.

Finishing these projects helps solidify Python's main ideas and provides useful experience for future programming.

I don't know about you, but learning gaming through coding or learning to code through gaming looks quite exciting to me. It's a win-win, isn't it? No matter what your dream is, you are well on your way to achieving it. Let us try our hands at these basic projects before you change the world.

The Rock-Paper-Scissors Game[lviii]

What is the rock-paper-scissors game?

We played rock-paper-scissors with our siblings or friends in our childhood. The main purpose of the game was to resolve the problem when there were limited resources or when young children had to make decisions. Everyone in the group would agree to play this game and accept the decision, as the decision made by this game felt unbiased and clear.

Never imagined playing this on computers, using program codes, but here we are. First of all, let's discuss the rules in case one is unfamiliar with the game.

- Rock-paper-scissors is a game played between two players using their hands.
- Players say "rock-paper-scissors" and then transform their hands together into:
    - Shape of a rock (fist)
    - Shape of scissors (two open fingers in a fist/victory sign but shown horizontally)
    - Shape of paper (open hand facing downward)
- The main idea is that:
    - rock can smash scissors (rock wins over scissors)
    - paper covers rock (paper wins over rock)
    - scissors cut paper (scissors wins over paper)

Now let's dive into the coding game.

 # Import the random module to simulate computer choices
import random

```
possible_options = ("rock", "paper", "scissors") # Creating a variable that holds the three options
player = None
computers_choice = random.choice(possible_options)  # Let the computer choose a random option by using choice() function

# The computer picks a random choice from options (rock, paper, scissors)
player = input ("Enter a choice((rock, paper, scissors): ")
print(f"Player: {player}")
print(f"Computer: {computers_choice}")
```

Output: Enter a choice (rock, paper, scissors): rock

Player: scissors

Computer: rock

The user will manually enter their choice of variable from rock, paper, or scissors. The computer will pick random choices from our possible_options. This part covers the computer and user input. Now we need to build it further to ensure only valid inputs are considered.

What if the player picks something that is not within the variable options? We would not want our program to take any random variables and continue to play the program. We need the user to pick a valid option only. Therefore, we will add a while loop for our input function:

import random
possible_options = ("rock", "paper", "scissors")
player = None
computers_choice = random.choice(possible_options)

while player not in possible_options:
    player = input ("Enter a choice (rock, paper, scissors): ")

print(f"Player: {player}")
print(f"Computer: {computers_choice}")

Output: Enter a choice (rock, paper, scissors): rocky

Enter a choice (rock, paper, scissors): balboa

Enter a choice (rock, paper, scissors): papor

Enter a choice (rock, paper, scissors): paper

Player: paper

Computer: rock

As you can see, we will be asked to input repeatedly until the input matches what is allowed from the list.

Now that we have this out of the way, let's get to the actual decision-making by adding if, elif options. Here is how I have done it. Leveraging the same code as above and adding the following to it:

```python
if player == computers_choice:
    print("Its a tie!")
elif player == "rock" and computers_choice == "scissors":
    print("You win!")
elif player == "paper" and computers_choice == "rock":
    print("You win!")
elif player == "scissors" and computers_choice == "paper":
    print("You win!")
else:
    print("You lose!")
```

Output

Enter a choice (rock, paper, scissors): rock

Player: rock

Computer: paper

You lose!

Enter a choice (rock, paper, scissors): rock

Player: rock

Computer: scissors

You win!

There are different ways this game can be coded. We have already seen in the example above how you can make modifications according to your preference. That's the beauty of it. After I wrote this code, I did a quick online search to see the least number of lines required to code this in Python. Take a guess. Four! Yes, just four lines of code. Was it the shortest? YES! Was it the most readable? NO! So, you can code it to be as long or as short as you want, but it's important to find the right balance between readability and conciseness.

That being said, don't worry about the number of lines in this project. The purpose is to get to the desired result for now, and we have done that.

Simple Calculator[lix]

It's time to do some math. Oh wait, are you not a numbers person? Don't worry, this program is going to help you crunch numbers like a pro. We are going to build a calculator. Isn't that exciting?

A calculator was like a magic toolbox when I was growing up. Unfortunately, my school didn't allow the use of calculators, and we had to do all the math in our head. I wish I knew programming then and would have built my own secret calculator.

In our project, we will leverage variables, operators, and functions to perform basic mathematical operations and solve equations. So, let's try our hand at creating a calculator using Python. Let's get started:

First of all, let's understand the requirements of the program:

- we need user inputs (num1 and num2); these will be our variables
- simple list of operations (+, -, *, /), basically four operators
- choice of statement: what the user wants to choose from the four operators (+, -, *, /)
- conditional statements (if, else, elif)

Here is how we could go about it:

while True: # This ensures that while the code inside the while loop is True, the program will keep on running. Only when the user enters a certain input will the code exit the loop. This comes in handy for using the calculator repeatedly as opposed to running the program every time you need to do a calculation

```
    print('''
    + Add
    - Subtract
    * Multiply
    / Divide
    ''')
```

 # We are simply displaying the operators using the above print statement for the user's convenience

```
    number_1 = int(input("Enter the first value: "))
    # First value entered (since we use float it can take decimals as well
    number_2 = int(input("Enter the second value: ")) Second value entered
    operator = input("Enter the operator of your choice (+, -, *, /): ")

    if operator == "+":
        print("Result: ", number_1 + number_2)
    elif operator == "-":
```

```python
        print("Result: ", number_1 - number_2)
    elif operator == "*":
        print("Result: ", number_1 * number_2)
    elif operator == "/":
        if number_2 == 0: # An additional if statement to ensure the calculator is not asked to perform an impossible calculation
            print("Error: Division by zero not possible!")
        else:
            print("Result: ", number_1 / number_2)
    else:
        print("operator invalid")

    calculate_again = input("Calculate again? (yes/no): ").lower() # Checking with the user if they want to calculate again
    if calculate_again == "no":
        break

print("Thank you for calculating!")
```

Output:

+ Add
- Subtract
* Multiply
/ Divide

Enter the first value: 100
Enter the second value: 50
Enter the operator of your choice (+, -, *, /): *
Result: 5000.0
Calculate again? (yes/no): yes

   + Add
   - Subtract
   * Multiply
   / Divide

Enter the first value: 100.50
Enter the second value: 2
Enter the operator of your choice (+, -, *, /): /
Result: 50.25
Calculate again? (yes/no): yes

   + Add
   - Subtract
   * Multiply
   / Divide

Enter the first value: 100
Enter the second value: 0
Enter the operator of your choice (+, -, *, /): /
Error: Division by zero not possible!
Calculate again? (yes/no): no
Thank you for calculating!

You might have noticed the use of lower() in the code above. Python is case-sensitive. So, when a user is asked to calculate again, if they enter "yes" or "no" in upper case or partial upper case, Python would treat that as an invalid input. Adding lower() helps Python convert everything to lowercase and then continue.

The Mad Libs Game[lx]

Remember your bedtime stories or the tales you read in books? The descriptions of people, places, objects, etc. made the stories or tales memorable. As much as I loved reading books, I could never become that articulate in writing. That's why I stick to writing books on technical content.

You might have heard of the Mad Libs game. We are going to use Python to help us play this game. In Mad Libs, you use your imagination to fill in missing words and create a hilarious story. To give you a simple example, a line from Mad Libs would look something like this:

May the _____ be with you!

You could fill in the blank with anything you like. You may choose "Force" to make it "May the Force be with you!"

I choose Unicorns, so the line becomes "May the Unicorns be with you!"

People play the game by using different words to describe the same thing. I am sure if you ask your friends, they'll come up with even funnier versions. We will add inputs such as nouns, verbs, adverbs, adjectives, etc., for the story formation. It's like filling in the blanks and completing a story game. Our Mad Libs game will use string manipulation to ask users for different words and create fun stories.

This specific project will help us get used to variables and strings. We will have the user input words as nouns, adjectives, etc. And then we want to insert these words into sentences. This project will help us get familiarized with the variables and strings.

Let's get started. First, you'll see the original story, followed by the code, which will help switch some nouns, verbs, and adjectives. While this won't be the best story you have ever read, it will surely give you a good idea of how to build a Mad Libs program in Python.

Story:

Two toddlers were playing in the park with their parents. The elder one started plucking leaves and flowers from the garden. All of a sudden they stumbled upon a cat and started laughing and clapping. The cat, startled by their action, started moving away from the two toddlers. The toddlers started chasing the cat. The cat jumped into the bushes and vanished. The sad toddlers came back to narrate the incident to their parents.

Code:

```
noun = input("Noun (plural): ")
noun2 = input("Noun2: ")
noun3 = input("Noun3: ")
verb = input("Verb (verb with an 'ing'): ")
verb2 = input("Verb2 (verb with an 'ing'): ")
verb3 = input("Verb3 (verb with an 'ing'): ")
verb4 = input("Verb4: ")
adjective = input("Adjective: ") # We will manually remove the words from the story paragraph below and replace it with verb, noun, and adjective words.

madlibs = "Two "+ noun +" and their parents were "+ verb +" in the park. The elder one started "+ verb2 +" in the garden. All of a sudden they stumbled upon a "+ noun2 +" and started "+ verb3 +" and clapping. While the "+ noun2 +", startled by their action, started moving away from the "+ noun +". The "+ noun +" started "+ verb4 +" with the "+ noun2 +". The "+ noun2 +" jumped into the bushes and vanished. The "+
```

adjective +" "+ noun +" came back to narrate the incident to their parents"

print(madlibs)

Output:

Noun (plural): Dogs
Noun2: Lion
Noun3: Elephant
Verb (verb with an 'ing'): eating
Verb2 (verb with an 'ing'): dancing
Verb3 (verb with an 'ing'): fighting
Verb4: climbing
Adjective: wonderful

Two Dogs and their parents were eating in the park. The elder one started dancing in the garden. All of a sudden they stumbled upon a Lion and started fighting and clapping. While the Lion, startled by their action, started moving away from the Dogs. The Dogs started climbing with the Lion. The Lion jumped into the bushes and vanished. The wonderful Dogs came back to narrate the incident to their parents

The output can be whatever you want it to be. So next time you get together with your friends and happen to be playing Mad Libs on paper and ink, you can introduce them to your state-of-the-art code. Wouldn't that be something?

Final Words

We come to an end of what has been quite a journey for you and me. I hope you were able to grasp all the important concepts discussed. Remember, in the world of coding, there is always a way to write something more efficiently, effectively, and beautifully. So, experiment fearlessly and embrace Python wholeheartedly.

This skill will last you a lifetime, allowing you to shape the future. So, next time you see any application, think whether building it in Python would be possible or not.

Respectfully,

A. R.

Before You Go…

I would be so very grateful if you would take a few seconds and rate or review this book on Amazon! Reviews – testimonials of your experience - are critical to an author's livelihood. While reviews are surprisingly hard to come by, they provide the life blood for me being able to stay in business and dedicate myself to the thing I love the most, writing.

If this book helped, touched, or spoke to you in any way, please leave me a review and give me your honest feedback.

Also, don't forget to pick up your gift, The Art of Asking Powerful Questions. Visit www.albertrutherford.com for further details.

Thank you so much for reading this book!

About the Author

Albert Rutherford

We're often blind to the root causes of our problems. Our attempts to resolve them are sometimes based on assumptions, misguided analyses, and incorrect conclusions, leading to misunderstandings, stress, and strain in both personal and professional relationships.

Before drawing conclusions, pause and reflect. Strive for accurate and consistent evaluation of information to make informed decisions. Embracing systems and critical thinking can enhance your proficiency in gathering and assessing data, paving the way for effective solutions in any situation.

Albert Rutherford has devoted his life to uncovering the best evidence-based strategies for superior decision-making. He lives by the creed, "ask better questions to uncover more precise answers and gain deeper insights."

Outside of his professional endeavors, Rutherford pursues his long-held aspiration of becoming an author. He cherishes moments with his family, stays updated with the latest scientific publications, enjoys fishing, and dabbles in the world of wines. Anchoring his belief in Benjamin Franklin's saying, "An investment in knowledge always pays the best interest," Rutherford continues his lifelong journey of learning.

Read more books from Albert Rutherford:

[Advanced Thinking Skills](#)

[The Systems Thinker Series](#)

[Game Theory Series](#)

[Critical Thinking Skills](#)

Reference List

Ankur. (2023, March 19). How to Create Mad Libs game in Python - Python Scholar. Python Scholar. Retrieved November 20, 2023, from https://pythonscholar.com/python-projects/mad-libs-game-in-python/

Badugu, P. (2023, May 4). *Python functions.* GeeksforGeeks. https://www.geeksforgeeks.org/python-functions/

Besbes, A. (2022, January 17). *How to use a variable number of arguments in Python functions.* Medium. https://towardsdatascience.com/how-to-use-variable-number-of-arguments-in python-functions-d3a49a9b7db6

Campbell, S. (2023, November 11). *Python variables: How to define/declare string variable types*. Guru 99. https://www.guru99.com/variables-in-python.html

Cassell, L., & Gauld, A. (2015). Python standard modules. In *Python projects* (1st ed., pp. 319-326). John Wiley & Sons, Inc.

Cesar, P. L. (2022, July 30). *Python basic syntax with examples and PDF*. IT Source Code. https://itsourcecode.com/python-tutorial/python-basic-syntax/

Chris, K. (2022, March 16). *Python functions – how to define and call a function.* Free Code Camp.

https://www.freecodecamp.org/news/python-functions-define-and-call-a-function/

Dixit, A. (2022, October 17). *Python file input/output: Read & write files in Python*. Data Science Central. https://www.datasciencecentral.com/python-file-input-output-read write-files-in-python/

Getting started using Python on Windows for beginners. (2023, March 9). Microsoft. Retrieved November 20, 2023, from https://learn.microsoft.com/en-us/windows/python/beginners

Grace, A. (n.d.). *Python continue – controlling for and while loops*. LearnDataSci. https://www.learndatasci.com/solutions/python-continue/

How to create Mad Libs game in Python. (n.d.). Python Scholar.

https://pythonscholar.com/python-projects/mad-libs-game-in-python/

How to distinguish between a variable and an identifier. (2019, August 1). Edureka!. Retrieved November 20, 2023, from https://www.edureka.co/community/53766/how-to-distinguish_between-a-variable-and-an-identifier

Hule, V. (2021, April 24a). *Check user input is a number or string in Python.* PYNative.

https://pynative.com/python-check-user-input-is-number-or-string/

Hule, V. (2021, July 25b). *Python control flow statements and loops.* PYNative.

https://pynative.com/python-control-flow-statements/

Input-output and files in Python (Python open, read and write to file). (2023, June 22). Software Testing Help. https://www.softwaretestinghelp.com/python/input-output-python-files/

Jaiswal, S. (2023, April). *Python data structures tutorial.* Data Camp. https://www.datacamp.com/tutorial/data-structures-python

Joshi, S. (2023, July 14). *51 latest WhatsApp marketing statistics for 2023: A deep dive.* Cooby. https://www.cooby.co/post/whatsapp-marketing-statistics

Kanungo, S. (n.d.). *Chapter 7: Zen of Python.* Primerlabs. https://primerlabs.io/chapters/zen-of-python/

Klein, B. (2023, November 8). *Modular programming and modules.* Python-Course EU. https://python-course.eu/python-tutorial/modules-and-modular-programming.php

Kshatriya, S. S. (n.d.). *The types of collections in Python.* Educative. https://www.educative.io/answers/the-types-of-collections-in-python

Kumari, K. (2023, August 14). *Understanding mutable and immutable in Python.* Great Learning. https://www.mygreatlearning.com/blog/understanding-mutable-and immutable-in-python/

Kumar, P. (2019, May 24). *Identifiers in Python – rules, examples & best practices*. Ask Python. https://www.askpython.com/python/python-identifiers-rules-best-practices

Manoj. (2023, July 29). *Python syntax – the complete guide*. IntelliPaat. https://intellipaat.com/blog/tutorial/python-tutorial/python-syntax/

Metz, C. (2015, September 16). *Google is 2 billion lines of code – and it's all in one place*. Wired. https://www.wired.com/2015/09/google-2-billion-lines-codeand-one-place/

NASA. (n.d.). *Mariner 1*. https://science.nasa.gov/mission/mariner-1/

Ostrowska, K. (2022, June 20). *A brief history of Python*. Learn Python.

https://learnpython.com/blog/history-of-python/

Oxford English Dictionary. (2007). Python. In *Oxford English Dictionary*. Retrieved November 20, 2023, from https://www.oed.com/dictionary/python_n1?tab=factsheet&tl=true#27300323

Pankaj. (2022, August 3). *Python data types (with complete list).* Digital Ocean. https://www.digitalocean.com/community/tutorials/python-data-types

Python. (2023, October 2). *Python 3.12.0.* https://www.python.org/downloads/release/python3120/

Python modules. (n.d.). Programiz. https://www.programiz.com/python-programming/modules

Python. (n.d. -a). *Built-in functions.* https://docs.python.org/3/library/functions.html

Python. (n.d. -b). *Using Python on Unix platforms.* https://docs.python.org/3/using/unix.html

Python program to make a simple calculator. (n.d.). Programiz. https://www.programiz.com/python-programming/examples/calculator

Python syntax – take your first step in the Python programming world. (n.d.). Data Flair. https://data-flair.training/blogs/python-syntax-semantics/

Python – variable types. (n.d.). Tutorials Point. https://www.tutorialspoint.com/python/python_variable_types.htm

Scikit-learn explained. (2023, September 15). AI-Jobs. https://ai-jobs.net/insights/scikit-learn explained/

Sturtz, J. (n.d.). *Conditional statements in Python.* Real Python. https://realpython.com/python conditional-statements/

Text files and binary files. (n.d.). Future Learn. https://www.futurelearn.com/info/courses/ programming-103-data/0/steps/64743

Top 10 reasons why Python is so popular with developers in 2023. (2022, September 28). UpGrad. https://www.upgrad.com/blog/reasons-why-python-popular-with-developers/

Understanding positional arguments in Python. (2019, February 15). Stack Overflow. Retrieved November 20, 2023, from https://stackoverflow.com/questions/54709025/understanding-positional-arguments-in-python

W3 Schools. (n.d. -a). *Python string methods.* https://www.w3schools.com/python/python_ref_string.asp

W3 Schools. (n.d. -b). *Python – variable names.* https://www.w3schools.com/python/python_variables_names.asp

What are identifiers in Python?. (n.d.). Flexiple. https://flexiple.com/python/identifiers-in-python

Wilkerson, C. (n.d.). *Make your first Python game: Rock, paper, scissors!.* Real Python. https://realpython.com/python-rock-paper-scissors/

Zaczynski, B. (n.d.). *Your guide to the Python print() function.* Real Python. https://realpython.com/python-print/

Endnotes

---

[i] 2018 Survey: SAS, R, or Python Preference for Data Pros (burtchworks.com), https://blog.burtchworks.com/industry-insights/2018-sas-r-or-python-survey-results-which-do-data-scientists-analytics-pros-prefer

ii Top Programming Languages 2022 - IEEE SpectrumNew Text file, https://spectrum.ieee.org/top-programming-languages-2022

[iii] *Top 10 reasons why Python is so popular with developers in 2023*. (2022, September 28). UpGrad. https://www.upgrad.com/blog/reasons-why-python-popular-with-developers/

[iv] Ostrowska, K. (2022, June 20). A brief history of Python. Learn Python. https://learnpython.com/blog/history-of-python/

[v] Getting started using Python on Windows for beginners. (2023, March 9). Microsoft. Retrieved November 20, 2023, from https://learn.microsoft.com/en-us/windows/python/beginners.

[vi] Python. (n.d. -b). Using Python on Unix platforms. https://docs.python.org/3/using/unix.htmll

[vii] Python. (2023, October 2). Python 3.12.0. https://www.python.org/downloads/release/python-3120/

[viii] Manoj. (2023, July 29). Python syntax – the complete guide. IntelliPaat. https://intellipaat.com/blog/tutorial/python-tutorial/python-syntax/

ix Metz, C. (2015, September 16). Google is 2 billion lines of code – and it's all in one place. Wired. https://www.wired.com/2015/09/google-2-billion-lines-

codeand-one-place/
[x] Python syntax – take your first step in the Python programming world. (n.d.). Data Flair. https://data-flair.training/blogs/python-syntax-semantics/
[xi] Python syntax – take your first step in the Python programming world. (n.d.). Data Flair. https://data-flair.training/blogs/python-syntax-semantics/
[xii] Cesar, P. L. (2022, July 30). Python basic syntax with examples and PDF. IT Source Code. https://itsourcecode.com/python-tutorial/python-basic-syntax/
[xiii] Python syntax – take your first step in the Python programming world. (n.d.). Data Flair. https://data-flair.training/blogs/python-syntax-semantics/
[xiv] Cesar, P. L. (2022, July 30). Python basic syntax with examples and PDF. IT Source Code. https://itsourcecode.com/python-tutorial/python-basic-syntax/
[xv] Cesar, P. L. (2022, July 30). Python basic syntax with examples and PDF. IT Source Code. https://itsourcecode.com/python-tutorial/python-basic-syntax/
[xvi] What are identifiers in Python?. (n.d.). Flexiple. https://flexiple.com/python/identifiers-in-python
[xvii] Kumar, P. (2019, May 24). Identifiers in Python – rules, examples & best practices. Ask Python. https://www.askpython.com/python/python-identifiers-rules-best-practices
[xviii] W3 Schools. (n.d. -b). Python – variable names. https://www.w3schools.com/python/python_variables_names.asp
[xix] How to distinguish between a variable and an identifier. (2019, August 1). Edureka!. Retrieved November 20, 2023, from https://www.edureka.co/community/53766/how-to-distinguish-between-a-variable-and-an-identifier
[xx] Campbell, S. (2023, November 11). Python variables: How

to define/declare string variable types. Guru 99. https://www.guru99.com/variables-in-python.html
[xxi] Python – variable types. (n.d.). Tutorials Point. https://www.tutorialspoint.com/python/python_variable_types.htm
[xxii] Kanungo, S. (n.d.). Chapter 7: Zen of Python. Primerlabs. https://primerlabs.io/chapters/zen-of-python/
[xxiii] Campbell, S. (2023, November 11). Python variables: How to define/declare string variable types. Guru 99. https://www.guru99.com/variables-in-python.html
[xxiv] Sturtz, J. (n.d.). Conditional statements in Python. Real Python. https://realpython.com/python-conditional-statements/
[xxv] Hule, V. (2021, July 25b). Python control flow statements and loops. PYNative. https://pynative.com/python-control-flow-statements/
[xxvi] Hule, V. (2021, April 24a). Check user input is a number or string in Python. PYNative. https://pynative.com/python-check-user-input-is-number-or-string/
[xxvii] Grace, A. (n.d.). Python continue – controlling for and while loops. LearnDataSci. https://www.learndatasci.com/solutions/python-continue/
[xxviii] Hule, V. (2021, April 24a). Check user input is a number or string in Python. PYNative. https://pynative.com/python-check-user-input-is-number-or-string/
[xxix] Hule, V. (2021, April 24a). Check user input is a number or string in Python. PYNative. https://pynative.com/python-check-user-input-is-number-or-string/
[xxx] W3 Schools. (n.d. -a). Python string methods. https://www.w3schools.com/python/python_ref_string.asp
[xxxi] W3 Schools. (n.d. -a). Python string methods. https://www.w3schools.com/python/python_ref_string.asp
[xxxii] Pankaj. (2022, August 3). Python data types (with complete list). Digital Ocean. https://www.digitalocean.com/community/tutorials/python-data-types

[xxxiii] Jaiswal, S. (2023, April). Python data structures tutorial. Data Camp. https://www.datacamp.com/tutorial/data-structures-python

[xxxiv] NASA. (n.d.). Mariner 1. https://science.nasa.gov/mission/mariner-1/

[xxxv] Jaiswal, S. (2023, April). Python data structures tutorial. Data Camp. https://www.datacamp.com/tutorial/data-structures-python

[xxxvi] Kumari, K. (2023, August 14). Understanding mutable and immutable in Python. Great Learning. https://www.mygreatlearning.com/blog/understanding-mutable-and-immutable-in-python/

[xxxvii] Pankaj. (2022, August 3). Python data types (with complete list). Digital Ocean. https://www.digitalocean.com/community/tutorials/python-data-types

[xxxviii] Oxford English Dictionary. (2007). Python. In Oxford English Dictionary. Retrieved November 20, 2023, from https://www.oed.com/dictionary/python_n1?tab=factsheet&tl=true#27300323.

[xxxix] Jaiswal, S. (2023, April). Python data structures tutorial. Data Camp. https://www.datacamp.com/tutorial/data-structures-python

[xl] Kshatriya, S. S. (n.d.). *The types of collections in Python.* Educative. https://www.educative.io/answers/the-types-of-collections-in-python

[xli] Joshi, S. (2023, July 14). 51 latest WhatsApp marketing statistics for 2023: A deep dive. Cooby. https://www.cooby.co/post/whatsapp-marketing-statistics

[xlii] Chris, K. (2022, March 16). Python functions – how to define and call a function. Free Code Camp. https://www.freecodecamp.org/news/python-functions-define-and-call-a-function/

[xliii] Python. (n.d. -a). Built-in functions. https://docs.python.org/3/library/functions.html

[xliv] Badugu, P. (2023, May 4). Python functions.

GeeksforGeeks. https://www.geeksforgeeks.org/python-functions/

[xlv] Chris, K. (2022, March 16). Python functions – how to define and call a function. Free Code Camp. https://www.freecodecamp.org/news/python-functions-define-and-call-a-function/

[xlvi] Understanding positional arguments in Python. (2019, February 15). Stack Overflow. Retrieved November 20, 2023, from https://stackoverflow.com/questions/54709025/understanding-positional-arguments-in-python

[xlvii] Besbes, A. (2022, January 17). How to use a variable number of arguments in Python functions. Medium. https://towardsdatascience.com/how-to-use-variable-number-of-arguments-in-python-functions-d3a49a9b7db6

[xlviii] Dixit, A. (2022, October 17). Python file input/output: Read & write files in Python. Data Science Central. https://www.datasciencecentral.com/python-file-input-output-read-write-files-in-python/

[xlix] Input-output and files in Python (Python open, read and write to file). (2023, June 22). Software Testing Help. https://www.softwaretestinghelp.com/python/input-output-python-files/

[l] Dixit, A. (2022, October 17). Python file input/output: Read & write files in Python. Data Science Central. https://www.datasciencecentral.com/python-file-input-output-read-write-files-in-python/

[li] Dixit, A. (2022, October 17). Python file input/output: Read & write files in Python. Data Science Central. https://www.datasciencecentral.com/python-file-input-output-read-write-files-in-python/

[lii] Text files and binary files. (n.d.). Future Learn. https://www.futurelearn.com/info/courses/programming-103-data/0/steps/64743

[liii] Zaczynski, B. (n.d.). Your guide to the Python print() function. Real Python. https://realpython.com/python-

print/

[liv] Klein, B. (2023, November 8). Modular programming and modules. Python-Course EU. https://python-course.eu/python-tutorial/modules-and-modular-programming.php

[lv] Python modules. (n.d.). Programiz. https://www.programiz.com/python-programming/modules

[lvi] Cassell, L., & Gauld, A. (2015). Python standard Modules. Retrieved November 20, 2023, from https://doi.org/10.1002/9781119207580.app2

[lvii] Scikit-learn explained. (n.d.). ai-jobs.net. Retrieved November 20, 2023, from https://ai-jobs.net/insights/scikit-learn-explained/

[lviii] Python, R. (2023, November 6). Make your first Python game: rock, paper, scissors! Retrieved November 20, 2023, from https://realpython.com/python-rock-paper-scissors/

[lix] Python program to make a simple calculator. (n.d.). Programiz. Retrieved November 20, 2023, from https://www.programiz.com/python-programming/examples/calculator

[lx] Ankur. (2023, March 19). How to Create Mad Libs game in Python - Python Scholar. Python Scholar. Retrieved November 20, 2023, from https://pythonscholar.com/python-projects/mad-libs-game-in-python/

Printed in Great Britain
by Amazon